Research Report
May 2011

CONSORTIUM ON CHICAGO SCHOOL RESEARCH AT THE UNIVERSITY OF CHICAGO

Student and Teacher Safety in Chicago Public Schools
The Roles of Community Context and School Social Organization

Matthew P. Steinberg, Elaine Allensworth, and David W. Johnson

Acknowledgements

The authors would like to acknowledge the many people who helped make this report possible. Many of our colleagues at the Consortium on Chicago School Research (CCSR) at the University of Chicago Urban Education Institute were crucial in developing and refining our findings at each stage of this project. This study began under the initiative and leadership of John Easton, former Director of CCSR, and it is because of him that we undertook and continued this line of work. Todd Rosenkranz provided invaluable assistance on data issues through all stages of the project; he prepared the data on which the empirical analysis was conducted and answered questions throughout the project about the quantitative data. Emily Krone provided very thoughtful comments and suggestions on the organization of this report. CCSR directors provided very helpful feedback on the work. In particular, Melissa Roderick encouraged us to combine qualitative findings from the Focus on Freshmen project with the quantitative analysis of data on safety. CCSR Steering Committee members Lila Leff, Peter Martinez, and Arie van der Ploeg reviewed the penultimate draft and also provided very helpful suggestions for revisions. CCSR Research Analyst Jim Murphy performed a very thorough technical read on the final draft.

We offer particular thanks to the other members of the Focus on Freshmen team who gathered data on the schools used as case studies, including David Stevens, Amber Stitziel Pareja, Desmond Patton, Melissa Roderick, Eric Brown, Marisol Mastrangelo, and Angela Garcia. We are especially grateful for the work of Desmond Patton, whose analysis of two students at "Lake Erie High School" is reproduced in this report.

We are very appreciative of the Spencer Foundation for providing core funding to CCSR that allows us to do work that is not project-based. Without this core support, this study would not have been possible. We thank the Carnegie Corporation of New York for funding the Focus on Freshmen study, from which the case studies were drawn.

Table of Contents

Executive Summary 1

Introduction 5

Chapter 1: *Issues of Safety in Chicago Schools* 13

Chapter 2: *Safety by Type of School and Neighborhood* 21

Chapter 3: *Safety by Internal School Organization and Practices* 33

Chapter 4: *Interpretive Summary* 45

References 49

Appendix A: *Student and Teacher Survey Responses* 52

Appendix B: *Survey Measures Used in This Report* 55

Appendix C: *Methodological Details on Statistical Models* 59

Appendix D: *Models of Safety by Neighborhood and School Context* ... 61

Endnotes 63

Executive Summary

In schools across the country, students routinely encounter a range of safety issues—from overt acts of violence and bullying to subtle intimidation and disrespect. Though extreme incidents such as school shootings tend to attract the most attention, day-to-day incidents such as gossip, hallway fights, and yelling matches between teachers and students contribute to students' overall sense of safety and shape the learning climate in the school. Not surprisingly, schools serving students from high-crime, high-poverty areas find it particularly challenging to create safe, supportive learning environments. Chicago Public Schools (CPS), the subject of this report, is no exception. In many CPS schools, teachers, and students report feeling unsafe in hallways, classrooms, and the area just outside the school building. Yet, in many other Chicago schools—even some schools serving large populations of students from high-poverty, high-crime areas—students and teachers do feel safe. What distinguishes these schools? This report shows that it is the quality of relationships between staff and students and between staff and parents that most strongly defines safe schools. Indeed, disadvantaged schools with high-quality relationships actually feel safer than advantaged schools with low-quality relationships.

Two years ago, CPS leadership suggested an innovative method of addressing safety concerns in schools—creating and implementing a "culture of calm" initiative predicated on developing positive and engaging relationships between adults and children. Though not an evaluation of culture of calm, this report provides initial evidence about the potential promise of such a strategy. The report examines the internal and external conditions that matter for students' and teachers' feelings of safety. It shows how the external conditions around the school, and in students' backgrounds and home communities, strongly define the level of safety in schools. It then examines

> It is the quality of relationships between staff and students and between staff and parents that most strongly defines safe schools.

CONSORTIUM ON CHICAGO SCHOOL RESEARCH AT THE UNIVERSITY OF CHICAGO the extent to which factors under the control of schools—their social and organizational structure, and particularly the relationships among adults and students—mediate those external influences.

Chapter 1 shows the aspects of the school environment that students and teachers consider of greatest concern in Chicago. Across CPS, the vast majority of students feel safe in their classrooms, but less safe in areas that lack adult supervision. Only about half of students feel safe in the area right outside their school. In fact, the area outside the school is even more problematic for students than the route they travel between home and school. In addition, only about half of CPS students say their peers treat each other with respect. Crime and disorder in schools are serious concerns for teachers as well as students, and this is especially true at the high school level, where more than half of teachers report problems associated with robbery or theft in the school, and over 60 percent report problems with gang activity and physical conflicts among students. While these statistics provide a sobering picture of the district, not all schools face serious problems with safety. Some schools provide very safe learning environments, while other schools struggle with extremely severe problems of disorder, aggression, and violence.

Chapter 2 identifies the types of schools in Chicago that struggle the most with problems of safety. It shows the ways in which neighborhood poverty, crime, and social resources are related to school safety, along with differences in safety by school racial composition and students' academic skills. Schools located in areas with high crime rates and substantial poverty tend to be less safe than schools located in more advantaged areas. However, it is not crime and poverty in the neighborhood of the school that matters for school safety as much as crime and poverty in students' home neighborhoods (which frequently differ from the neighborhood of the school). Schools tend to be safer the more that their students come from communities with less poverty and crime, and especially where there are social resources in the community. The schools serving students from neighborhoods with the highest crime rates and the fewest social resources predominantly serve African American students; thus, most of the schools with the worst safety are African American schools.

While it seems natural to focus on crime and poverty as the characteristics most strongly associated with school safety, another feature of school composition is a much stronger determinant of safety: the degree to which the school enrolls high-achieving versus low-achieving students. After accounting for the incoming academic achievement of the school's students, there is effectively no relationship between crime and poverty and school safety. Crime and poverty are related to school safety largely because students living in high-poverty, high-crime neighborhoods are more likely than children from other areas to enter school with low academic achievement. Schools that enroll more students who have struggled in school in the past are more likely to have problems with safety and order. This suggests that schools serving students with low achievement must closely attend to issues of safety if they are to have a climate conducive to learning and reduce their achievement gap. Yet, this does not suggest more emphasis on punitive discipline approaches, especially for low-achieving students who are already less likely than others to be comfortable and engaged in school. Rather, as shown in Chapter 3, it suggests that schools serving a large number of low-achieving students must make stronger efforts to foster trusting, collaborative relationships with students and their parents.

Chapter 3 investigates the ways in which internal school organizational factors explain the differences in safety among schools serving very similar student populations, and mediate the adverse influences of community poverty and crime. The relationships that teachers and school personnel foster with students, and the interactions they have with families, play important roles in insulating students from adverse neighborhood conditions and creating safe schooling environments. In contrast to the positive role that relationship-building plays in fostering safe schooling environments, high rates of student suspensions do not show any benefit. In fact, schools with high suspension rates are less safe than schools with lower suspension rates, even when they serve similar students from similar types of neighborhoods.

The findings from this report point to the important role that school leaders and personnel can play in fostering safe schooling environments, even in schools that serve students from disadvantaged neighborhoods. While schools may not be able to entirely overcome adverse neighborhood influences, the adults in the school building can promote structures and relationships that mediate them. Specifically, school leaders should be aware of the places in the school building that students feel least safe—for example, the areas just outside and around the school—and increase the adult presence in response to students' concerns. In addition to the presence of adults, the nature and quality of the interactions between adults and students matter greatly. But positive interactions do not just happen organically. Promoting positive interactions between students and adults requires concerted attention to the ways in which the school environment is structured. For example, training teachers and staff on how to deal with conflict in constructive ways could help prevent conflicts from escalating. The evidence also suggests critical analysis of the ways in which school personnel engage families in constructive and supportive ways. How do schools make families feel welcome in the school and make teachers feel that they have the support of parents? These are the critical questions to ask as schools strive to foster safer learning environments for children.

Introduction

There's fighting like—every Friday there's a fight . . . at our school . . . It make me feel distracted and stuff like that, nervous.

—Zalisha, ninth-grader at Lake Erie High School[1]

Every day, Zalisha goes to school in a chaotic environment, where fights break out regularly, and teachers struggle to maintain order in their classrooms. Not all students in Chicago attend schools as unsafe as Zalisha's school, but concerns about safety are prevalent among students and teachers at many schools across the district. This is a basic issue that has serious consequences for students' academic growth and personal well-being. In response, the district has suggested an innovative method of addressing this serious issue—creating and implementing a "culture of calm." The culture of calm is predicated on developing positive and engaging relationships between adults and children as a means of preventing disruptive behavior. This is in contrast to more punitive approaches, which are common in districts across the country and in Chicago schools. While not an evaluation of the culture of calm initiative, this report provides some initial evidence about the promise of such a strategy.

School safety is a pressing concern in Chicago and the nation, and there is a need for more information about the nature of the problem and the factors that mitigate or exacerbate problems. To date, little is known about the nature of the problem across schools, the reasons safety varies in different sites, or the features of schools that lead them to have better climates. This report provides new evidence on these issues.

> **Concerns about safety are prevalent among students and teachers at many schools across the district.**

- Chapter 1 shows the nature of the problem in Chicago—the degree to which students and teachers feel safe in their schools, and which aspects of the school environment are of greatest concern. This chapter provides information on which aspects of school safety are most in need of intervention, and the extent to which such interventions are needed in schools across the district.
- Chapter 2 identifies which types of schools struggle the most with problems of safety, and the ways in which school and neighborhood characteristics, such as poverty and crime, are related to school safety. This chapter has implications for how students are assigned to schools, and how to allocate resources and design effective strategies based on the types of students that the school serves and the neighborhoods in which they are located.
- Chapter 3 examines differences across schools in the way they function—the extent to which teachers, leaders, and parents collaborate, the focus on instruction, and the quality of leadership—as well as their use of suspensions for misbehavior, to determine what it is about schools, other than the students that they serve, that leads them to have very different climates. This chapter provides evidence about what really matters for school safety, and whether schools can overcome the negative influences that crime and poverty in the community have on safety.

A National Problem and Urban Crisis

The safety of America's students and schools periodically comes to the public's attention when shootings or homicides of school-aged children occur. The September 2009 beating death of CPS student Derrion Albert, in which four teenagers were subsequently charged with first-degree murder, made national headlines. Yet, physical attacks against public school students often occur without substantial attention in the media. Furthermore, not all of the threats that students face occur outside of the school building. In fact, the violent crime rate among public school students while at school is higher than the violent crime rate nationally among the general population.[2]

School safety is a particularly pressing issue in urban public schools; the incidence of violent episodes is almost 60 percent higher in city schools than in suburban schools, and 30 percent higher than in rural schools.[3] Urban schools are approximately twice as likely as other schools to report that students verbally abuse teachers and act disrespectfully (other than verbal abuse) toward teachers either daily or at least once a week.[4]

Extreme forms of violence, such as the school shootings that occurred at Columbine High School in the spring of 1999, are often sensationalized as a reflection of school safety and are mentioned frequently by politicians and media outlets. However, these events are rare and only one of many areas of concern for students and teachers. The daily interactions among students and their teachers that involve threats and intimidation—both physical and verbal—affect the academic performance of students and the effectiveness of teachers throughout the school year.

Student bullying, for example, generally commands less attention than school shootings but strongly affects students' school experience. Bullying behaviors include both physical forms of aggression (assault, stealing, or vandalizing a victim's property), and emotional forms of bullying (name calling, threats of violence, slandering, excluding the victim from group activities, and taunting). These physical and emotional forms of bullying often occur repeatedly and are intended to intimidate the victim and create a pattern of humiliation, fear, and abuse.[5]

Bullying often results from a lack of adult supervision in areas such as hallways, playgrounds, and lunchrooms, and evidence suggests that students feel most unsafe in unsupervised places in and around schools.[6] In the 2007–08 school year, 25 percent of all U.S. public schools reported occurrences of student bullying daily or at least once per week.[7] In a nationally representative survey of middle and high school age students, 65 percent of teens reported having been verbally or physically harassed or assaulted during the past year; reasons for such harassment include the student's perceived or actual appearance, gender, sexual orientation, gender expression, race/ethnicity, disability, or religion.[8] Bullying is particularly problematic among middle school–aged students, who report rates of bullying more than twice those of primary and high school students.[9]

Recent media attention has begun to focus on bullying and its effect on student welfare. The tragic suicide of Massachusetts teen Phoebe Prince in January 2010 brought national attention to the impact of physical and emotional bullying, as nine students were charged with acts ranging from statutory rape to violation of civil rights with bodily injury, criminal harassment, and stalking. In response to the growing concern over bullying, in August 2010 the U.S. Department of Education hosted its first summit on bullying, where assistant deputy secretary Kevin Jennings noted that "(bullying) can leave lifetime scars. And in the case of some of these young people, it can lead to their decision to end their own lives."[10]

Reasons for Concern

There are a number of reasons to be worried about students' feelings of safety in schools, not only from threats of physical violence but also from non-physical harassment. Students' emotional well-being is important in itself. But beyond the immediate emotional consequences, there are a number of short-term and long-term consequences of victimization. It affects student functioning in school, adversely impacting student self-efficacy, attitudinal and behavioral investments in education, and the amount of time in school dedicated to student learning, while also producing lower levels of academic achievement. Students who are victims of harassment attend school less frequently and feel less connected to and less engaged in school. In turn, they spend less time doing homework and participating in school activities, which ultimately has adverse effects on both cognitive and social growth.[11]

In the long-term, a link exists between youth victimization and more negative life outcomes. These include psychological and health problems, as well as disrupted educational and occupational attainment. These, in turn, negatively affect a student's later economic status, including labor force participation, occupational status, and earnings.[12] Student victimization and harassment while in school negatively impact academic and social functioning and ultimately shape a student's later life outcomes.

In addition, teachers are also affected by the extent of harassment and violence that occurs in schools. Unsafe school environments have adverse effects on teacher professional development and personal safety. Children who are physically and verbally abusive in the classroom divert teachers' attention away from teaching, preventing teachers from being able to teach effectively.[13] Teachers are also more likely to leave schools with substantial student disciplinary problems, which further decreases school capacity for effective instruction.[14]

Policy Efforts Addressing School Safety

In light of the increasing recognition of the negative impact that unsafe school environments have on students and teachers, policymakers at both the federal and local levels have attempted to address concerns around school safety. The federal government has provided funding for the Safe Schools/Healthy Students Initiative, a partnership between the U.S. Departments of Education, Health and Human Services, and Justice. This comprehensive approach to youth violence prevention is designed to prevent violence and substance abuse throughout U.S. schools and communities. The initiative distributed nearly $75 million in grant awards to school districts for the 2008–09 school year to "provide integrated and comprehensive resources for prevention programs and pro-social services for youth."[15] Underlining the importance of the initiative, U.S. Secretary of Education Arne Duncan said, "Every child in America deserves a safe and healthy school environment, and it's our job as educators, parents, and community members to ensure that happens."[16]

While it is imperative that schools establish a safe climate for students and teachers, it is less clear what strategies are most effective, especially in schools located in neighborhoods with high rates of crime and poverty and few human and social resources. One common response to concerns about safety and violence is to increase the overt presence of school security through the use of metal detectors and security guards. Nationally, 53 percent of U.S. public schools search student lockers, 54 percent lock entrance and/or exit doors during the school day, 90 percent place school staff in the hallways, and 93 percent require visitors to sign in upon entering the school building.[17]

Schools have also enacted "zero tolerance" policies. These policies employ major consequences, such as school suspension and expulsion, for even relatively minor infractions and do not allow for individual circumstances to be taken into account when determining punishment.[18] The theory is that tough, uniform enforcement of policies for all offenses will prevent more serious offenses from occurring. However, in practice, "zero tolerance" policies are often associated with higher levels of student fear at school, increased rates of school suspension, and loss of instructional time, with little if any evidence of a positive effect on reducing school violence.[19] Moreover, student suspensions and expulsions from school disproportionately affect economically disadvantaged students, students with emotional and behavioral disorders, and minority students.[20]

Teachers and administrators often respond to student disciplinary problems through office referrals, school suspension, and expulsion. In the 2005-06 school year, approximately 48 percent of all U.S. public schools (approximately 39,600 schools) took a severe disciplinary action against a student: either a school suspension lasting five or more days, expulsion, or transfer to specialized schools. Of the 830,700 serious disciplinary actions in 2005–06, 74 percent were suspensions for five days or more, 5 percent were school expulsions, and 20 percent were transfers to specialized schools.[21] In CPS, about 16 percent of students in grades six to eight were suspended in the 2008–09 school year, causing them to miss a week of school, on average (5.2 days). About 22 percent of CPS high school students were suspended in the same year, with an average suspension of over a week of school (6.6 days). Thus, large numbers of CPS students are missing a week or more of school due to disciplinary infractions.

In contrast to punitive responses to student misconduct, recent evidence suggests that meaningful relationships between teachers and students may play a role in lowering the incidence of student disciplinary infractions.[22] This perspective is consistent with the culture of calm initiative, which emphasizes the importance of developing safe, well-managed school environments in order to improve student safety and increase learning, while underscoring the centrality of respectful interactions and relationships among students and adults.[23]

Prior Research on School Safety

Prevailing research suggests that students' feelings of safety at school, and problems with peer relationships and bullying, are influenced by a broad array of factors, including students' own attributes, attributes of their schools, adults with whom students interact, families, neighborhoods, and the broader society.[24] A number of studies have shown that community-level factors, such as crime and poverty, while related to school safety, are not solely deterministic of school climate.[25] However, it remains largely unknown how school policies and practices mediate the influence of neighborhood and community-level factors on school safety. In particular, there is very little research on the ways in which the social-organizational structures of schools—internal, school-based resources and the interactions that occur among students, teachers, and parents—affect the climate of safety in schools.[26] This study provides empirical evidence on the role that school social-organizational structure plays in shaping safety in urban American schools.

A recent case study by Astor and colleagues of nine Israeli schools provides initial evidence on the internal school structures that influence the climate of safety.[27] This work showed that a number of organizational factors within schools—the nature of teacher-student relationships, the presence of clear procedures coupled with teacher belief in school procedures, a coherent school educational mission, and an influential and respected principal with strong relationships with teachers—mediate the effect of community influences on school safety. Their findings on the importance of leadership and cooperative work among teachers are consistent with theories of organizational change stating that school climate and learning depend on inclusive leadership with empowered stakeholders.[28] The importance of student-teacher relationships is also supported by sociological studies showing that schools are important settings for transmitting values related to violence to students and for the formation of social bonds with adults.[29] In particular, stronger intergenerational bonding—the relationships between students and adults—in school is associated with a lower likelihood of disciplinary problems.[30] Thus, the extent to which students feel supported by their teachers and view their teachers as supportive of their academic and social development can shape the level of social resources in schools, and, in turn, school safety.

Astor's case studies, together with the theoretical work, suggest that school leadership, as well as teacher collective effort and strong relationships with students, might be important mechanisms for mediating the influence of external factors on school safety. The work presented here builds on this theoretical and empirical literature. We employ a large sample of schools, rather than a small number of case studies, to examine the ways in which a school's social-organizational structure is related to school safety, given the social and economic context in which the school exists.

In addition to examining the potential mechanisms through which schools may foster safe schooling environments, this study leverages a unique dataset to capture safety across Chicago schools. We use reports from students in grades six through 12 and teachers in grades K–12 to capture three dimensions of safety.

From students' perspectives, we capture general feelings of safety in and around the school, as well as the nature of interactions among students in the school—the degree to which peers are respectful or mean to each other. From teachers' perspectives, we capture perceptions about crime and disorder in their schools. See the sidebar "How School Safety Is Measured in This Study" for details on the survey questions used to measure safety in this report. We also use case studies of two high schools to illustrate the issues shown with the surveys. As part of another CCSR research project, researchers spent time observing classrooms and public areas in these two schools, and interviewed students and teachers about their experiences. One of the schools provides a picture of a typical CPS high school in terms of safety (pseudonym: Huron), while the other is a particularly unsafe school (pseudonym: Lake Erie). We further contrast these schools with a third school where students and teachers feel very safe (pseudonym: Pacific), but for whom we do not have observational data. However, we do have reports from

---

Data Used in This Study

This study uses data from a number of different sources. Information on school safety comes from surveys of students and teachers, as described in the sidebar "How School Safety Is Measured in This Study." Surveys also provide information about the degree to which students feel there are supportive adults in their home communities. Information on school racial composition, size, percent of low-income students, and grade level comes from CPS student administrative files. Information on student achievement comes from CPS test files. For schools serving grades K–8, average achievement is based on the ISAT exam, which is taken in the spring in grades three through eight. For high schools, average achievement is based on the EXPLORE exam, which is taken in early October of the ninth-grade year. Information on the economic characteristics of neighborhoods comes from the 2000 U.S. Census at the block group level, while information on neighborhood crime comes from the records of the Chicago Police Department. Further details on the specific indicators used from these data sources are provided within the descriptions of findings. Quotes and observations of case study schools come from a qualitative study that examined differences in students' experiences in the ninth-grade year.

Case Study Methods

Qualitative data come from the Focus on Freshmen project, a study designed to understand the transition to high school. In the course of that study, researchers found that issues of safety and disorder were a large concern in a number of schools, affecting student attendance and their engagement in schoolwork. The study also showed that suspensions were a major source of course absence in some schools. We incorporate some of the findings from that study in this report because of the strong intersections between the two studies.

Data for the Focus on Freshmen study were gathered through in-depth, semi-structured interviews with 72 students between May 2008 and February 2010, first in four public elementary schools and later in five public high schools, at multiple time points across the transition from eighth grade to ninth grade. Using seventh-grade Illinois State Achievement Test (ISAT) math scores, we oversampled for middle-achieving students, excluding all students in the "academic warning" category and most from the "exceeds" category. For the high school case studies, we primarily include data from observations and interviews in two high schools, one with typical levels of safety and another with extremely problematic safety. None of the schools in the Focus on Freshmen project had above-average levels of safety.

Qualitative data were analyzed using typological analysis (Hatch, 2002; LeCompte and Preissle, 1993). Interviews were transcribed and entered into Atlas Ti qualitative software program. This process facilitated data management, allowing us to easily sort and retrieve data for further analysis. Working with general themes individually, we coded transcripts excerpts inductively for emerging patterns. After codes within themes were developed, we then created data displays (Miles and Huberman, 1994) summarizing each case along several relevant factors. These tables allowed us to see trajectories within cases, patterns across cases, and relationships between the factors we examined.

surveys of students and teachers about the climate at Pacific. These three schools highlight the very different types of environments that students experience in high schools across the city.

Some other studies have used data on school security responses to disorder, school disciplinary data (e.g., number of suspensions), and student and teacher self-reports of victimization to capture safety in schools.[31] However, there are a number of reasons to believe that these measures do not accurately depict school safety. Schools may over-report disciplinary infractions to appear vigilant in upholding school rules and order, or under-report disciplinary infractions so as to appear safer. Similarly, school security responses to crime and disorder may also be plagued by the same inherent biases found in school reports of suspensions. Schools may employ security measures (such as metal detectors and security guards) to demonstrate a hard line on school safety in a school where safety is not a major concern, or as a response to real concerns around the level of safety in the school. As such, we believe that student and teacher reports offer a more valid means of ascertaining the level of safety and disorder in schools. Reports from students and teachers about their perceptions of school climate may not be completely objective, as they are influenced by their own biases and backgrounds; however, they have the advantage of showing how people are actually interpreting their experiences in the school environment, and so may be highly accurate in terms of people's feelings and concerns about their school. Chapter 3 shows how suspension rates are related to student and teacher reports of safety in CPS schools.

How School Safety Is Measured in This Study

CCSR surveys were administered to students in grades six through 12 during the spring of 2007 and 2009. This report focuses on responses from spring 2009, but data from 2007 were also used to examine trends over the last few years and to check for response bias in 2009. Questions were asked around three aspects of safety. The first set of questions asks students to reflect on their general sense of personal safety inside and outside of the school and traveling to and from school (see Table A). A high score means they feel very safe in all of these areas. The second set of questions (referred to as "peer interactions") asks students if their classmates treat each other with respect, work together well, and help each other learn, and if other students like to put others down, and don't care about each other. In high-scoring schools, positive behaviors are prevalent, and the problematic, negative behaviors are less prevalent. When they were combined into one measure, the items that indicate negative behaviors were reversed so that higher scores on this measure indicate better peer relationships. The final set of questions measures the degree to which teachers perceive the existence of disorder and crime, such as theft, vandalism, and violence, in the school. Ordinarily, higher scores on this measure indicate a less safe environment, but we reversed the scores so that higher values represent a safer environment; this makes it easier to compare teacher responses with those of students.

TABLE A

Survey questions about school safety

CCSR Survey Measure	Survey Question
Student Perceptions of Safety (Surveys of students in grades six to 12)	**How Safe Do You Feel** (not safe; somewhat safe; mostly safe; very safe): 1. Outside around the school 2. Traveling between home and school 3. In the hallways and bathrooms of the school 4. In your classes
Student Perceptions of Peer Interactions (Surveys of students in grades six to 12)	**How Much Do You Agree With the Following Statements About Students in Your School** (strongly disagree; disagree; agree; strongly agree): *Most students in my school:* 1. Don't really care about each other 2. Like to put others down 3. Help each other learn 4. Don't get along together very well 5. Just look out for themselves 6. Treat each other with respect
Teacher Perceptions of Crime and Disorder (Surveys of teachers in grades K–12)	**To What Extent is Each of the Following a Problem at Your School** (not at all; a little; some; to a great extent): 1. Physical conflicts among students 2. Robbery or theft 3. Gang activity 4. Disorder in classrooms 5. Disorder in hallways 6. Student disrespect of teachers 7. Threats of violence toward teachers

Chapter 1

Issues of Safety in Chicago Schools

Many students and teachers in Chicago report serious concerns with safety, crime, and disorder in their schools. Students also report substantial issues with the quality of their peer relationships. This chapter reveals areas of particular concern to both students and teachers. It begins by describing three Chicago schools with three very different climates, drawing on reports from students on surveys, as well as interviews of students and teachers at two of those schools. The survey reports of these three schools are then put into the context of survey reports from students and teachers throughout the district to show the patterns of safety in schools across the city.

> Schools in Chicago vary considerably in the degree to which students and teachers feel they are safe.

Schools in Chicago vary considerably in the degree to which students and teachers feel they are safe. Table 1 highlights three high schools as examples. In one of the safer high schools, called Pacific[32] in this report, almost all students feel safe within the school building and the vast majority feel safe coming and going to school. Teachers report few problems with crime or violence—just occasional disorder in the hallways and some problems with robbery, but few problems with classroom disorder, fights, or disrespect of teachers. Most students say their peers get along well and care about each other, although only about half feel their peers are respectful to each other. In Pacific, only about 5 percent of students were suspended during the 2008–09 school year. In sum, Pacific provides a generally safe climate for teachers and students to work. Across the system, students at about one-quarter of all high schools and half of all elementary schools feel as safe, or even more safe, than Pacific students.

CONSORTIUM ON CHICAGO SCHOOL RESEARCH AT THE UNIVERSITY OF CHICAGO

TABLE 1

There are large differences in safety across high schools: three examples

	Student Perceptions of Safety	Teacher Perceptions of Crime and Disorder	Student Perceptions of Peer Interactions
Pacific A Safe High School	• 92% feel safe in classrooms • 90% feel safe in hallways and bathrooms • 63% feel safe traveling between home and school • 39% feel safe just outside the school	• 0% report violent threats to teachers • 31% report robbery/theft • 7% report gang activity • 11% report disorder in classrooms • 24% report disorder in the hallways • 7% report physical conflicts • 10% report disrespect of teachers	• 63% say peers help each other learn • 70% say peers care about each other • 66% say peers get along well together • 45% say peers just look out for themselves • 48% say peers treat each other with respect • 47% say peers put others down
Huron A Typical High School	• 83% feel safe in classrooms • 70% feel safe in hallways and bathrooms • 47% feel safe traveling between home and school • 35% feel safe just outside the school	• 16% report violent threats to teachers • 29% report robbery/theft • 75% report gang activity • 69% report disorder in classrooms • 73% report disorder in the hallways • 61% report physical conflicts • 62% report disrespect of teachers	• 61% say peers help each other learn • 60% say peers care about each other • 55% say peers get along well together • 58% say peers just look out for themselves • 45% say peers treat each other with respect • 46% say peers put others down
Lake Erie An Unsafe High School	• 60% feel safe in classrooms • 50% feel safe in hallways and bathrooms • 45% feel safe traveling between home and school • 30% feel safe just outside the school	• 75% report violent threats to teachers • 91% report robbery/theft • 95% report gang activity • 92% report disorder in classrooms • 93% report disorder in the hallways • 98% report physical conflicts • 98% report disrespect of teachers	• 56% say peers help each other learn • 42% say peers care about each other • 34% say peers get along well together • 66% say peers just look out for themselves • 31% say peers treat each other with respect • 63% say peers put others down

In a more typical CPS high school, like Huron (pseudonym), the vast majority of students feel safe within the building, but there are problems outside of the school building. Half of students are concerned about coming and going to school, and only about one-third feel safe in the area just outside the school.

The physical aspects of Huron appear conducive to teaching and learning.[33] A visitor entering the building would find it inviting, clean, and well maintained. Just inside the main doors, security guards greet students and visitors in fluid Spanish and English. During classes, hallways are usually empty and quiet. Groups of laughing and talking students walk together during a passing period, moving easily in wide hallways and stairwells.

However, teachers and students at Huron struggle with some serious issues around safety. As shown in Table 1, teachers report some problems with violent threats in the building, and many report problems associated with gang activity and fights. One student complains that at Huron there are *"gangbangers everywhere."* Occasionally, arguments reflecting underlying racial tensions between students erupt into fights, disrupting classes and hallways. Furthermore, more than

60 percent of teachers report problems with disorder and disrespect. When asked to describe his classmates' behavior in school, one Huron student observes that *"they're like animals—they like, run around the school, [the] class . . . they be throwing papers."* Less than half of students feel that peers are respectful to each other, and only 55 percent report that peers get along well together. Another Huron student complains that some of her classmates *"are gossipers . . . they start drama"* intentionally. Thus, despite a physical environment that is neat and orderly, students and teachers face intermittent threats, and classes often are not conducive to learning. Many high schools and elementary schools in Chicago have similar environments. However, Huron does have a better record than average in terms of student discipline. In 2008–09, only 16 percent of Huron students were suspended, which is typical among K–8 schools but low for high schools.

Lake Erie (pseudonym) is an example of one of the least safe high schools in the city. In this school, not only do students feel unsafe outside of the building, but half the students feel unsafe in the hallways and bathrooms and only 60 percent feel safe in their classrooms. Inside Lake Erie, the physical environment is dominated by crowd-control mechanisms: metal detectors, which are present throughout CPS high schools, greet students upon entering; folding tables corral students at the main entrance and at informal security *"checkpoints"* throughout hallways; folding metal gates are pulled across entrances to stairwells and padlocked. There is a constant police presence outside and inside the school.

Nearly all teachers at Lake Erie report problems with robbery in the building, gang activity, fights, disorder, and disrespect, and three-quarters of teachers report that students threaten them with violence. Interactions between students and teachers are frequently hostile and mutually disrespectful; students' and teachers' frustration with one another are easily visible. An algebra teacher at Lake Erie complains that constant disruption *"impedes the teaching process"*; repeated conflicts make it difficult, he continues, for teachers *"to reach students who want to learn as deeply as you know [they] could."* Another teacher observes, *"I see behavior problems I have never seen before . . . I get cursed out almost daily."* An English teacher describes how she tries to handle the fights that routinely disrupt her ninth-grade English class:

> I always throw the kids into the hall. . . one way or another I get the kids into the hall, because otherwise they destroy my room. They rip things off the walls, when they're rolling around they knock over the desks, the other kids get involved. . . And so as I get the fight into the hall, I lay myself back against the door, and that's how I keep the rest of the kids in the classroom. And that's kind of what we all do, the teachers against the door on the outside, you can keep the kids in the room. . . . [Once], I went back in [to the classroom] after [a] fight and [the students inside] were so irritated that I wouldn't let them out of the room that they cracked my oak podium in half.

The majority of students say their peers don't get along, just look out for themselves, put each other down, and don't treat each other with respect. Students at Lake Erie view arguments and fights as almost inevitable, even when they themselves work to avoid involvement. A female student at Lake Erie complains that:

> [other students] see a fight, and come out of the classroom [to watch]; then they get knocked out [too] . . . [I] can't get back in the classroom because they stepped out to watch a fight. [It seems like] they always start a fight when I'm going to [English class] . . . The next thing you know, I'm late [to class] and I get locked out [by the teacher.

Violence inside and outside the school creates a climate of mistrust, antagonism, and fear. Another student observes that, after being involved in a fight after school, he no longer walks in the hallways at school by himself. *"I make sure my brother is always with me now,"* he explains—for his own protection and *"[to] make sure they're always OK."* As one would expect, the suspension rate at Lake Erie is high compared with the system average; approximately one-third (34 percent) of Lake Erie students were suspended for at least one school day in 2008–09. Those who were suspended received, on average, nine days of suspension.

Figure 1 puts safety at Pacific, Huron, and Lake Erie in the context of all other CPS schools. The far-left position of Lake Erie shows that it is one of the bottom three schools in the system in terms of teachers' reports of safety. Thus, it is an extreme case, but not an isolated case. In terms of students' reports of safety, it is far from alone; there is a group of about 14 high schools, shown on the bottom left of Figure 1, in which students feel extremely unsafe. Huron has typical levels of safety from teachers' perspective—it is at the 50th percentile among all schools, and above-average among high schools. Students feel less safe at Huron than teachers, and this is largely because of concerns outside of the school building—as indicated in Table 1. The same is true at Pacific: While it is one of the five safest high schools from teachers' perspective, and in the top quarter of schools from students' perspective, concerns about safety outside of the building are a problem, especially in the area immediately outside of the school.

The Vast Majority of CPS Students Feel Safe in their Classrooms, but Less Safe in Areas with Little Adult Supervision

With some exceptions, the interior of the school building is a safe environment for most CPS students. Over 95 percent of CPS students say they feel at least somewhat safe in their classrooms (see Figure 2); over 80 percent say they feel mostly safe. This is consistent with other research that shows safety is affected by adult supervision. The vast majority of CPS students also feel at least somewhat safe in the hallways and bathrooms of their school. These are areas with less adult supervision, but where adults are close by.

CPS students feel least safe in the area just outside of the school.[34] Only about half of students in CPS elementary and high schools say they mostly feel safe in the area around the school. Approximately one-third of students are also concerned about their safety while

FIGURE 1

Student and teacher reports of safety tend to correspond with each other

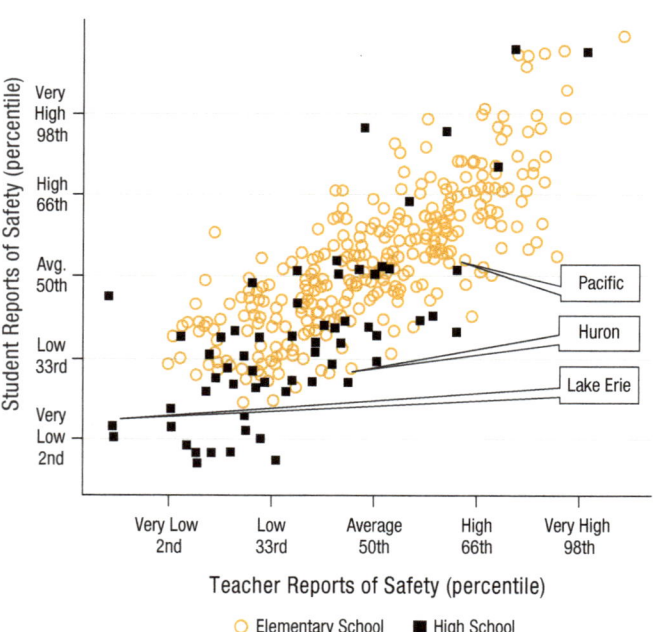

Note: Each dot represents a single school. Safer schools are in the upper right portion of the distribution and unsafe schools are in the bottom left portion of the distribution. "Very Low" represents two standard deviations below the mean (about the 2nd percentile). "Low" represents one standard deviation below the mean (about the 33rd percentile). "Average" is the 50th percentile. "High" is one standard deviation above the mean (about the 66th percentile). "Very High" is two standard deviations above the mean (about the 98th percentile). There are 62 high schools and 310 elementary schools represented in the graph.

FIGURE 2

Student reports of safety in and around their school

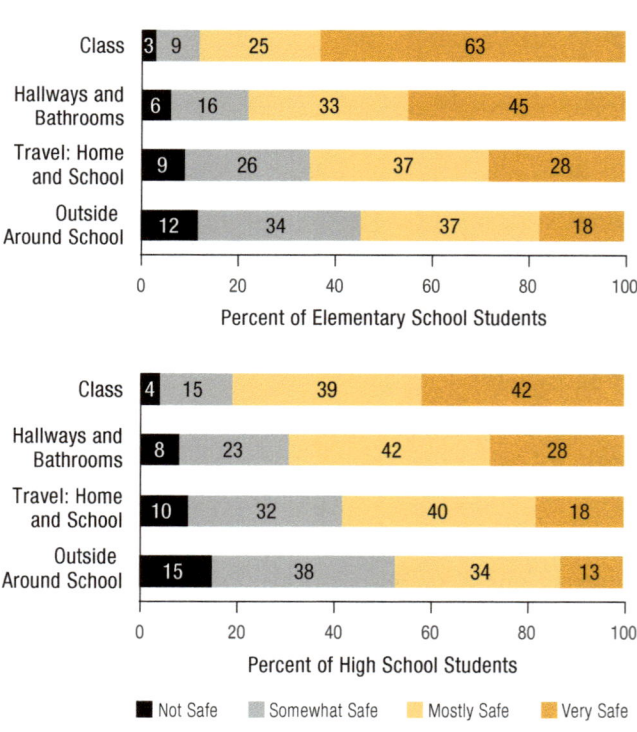

Note: See Appendix A for details about the sample of teacher and student respondents and response rates, and about the representativeness of the survey responses for all CPS students and teachers.

FIGURE 3

Student reports of peer interactions at their school

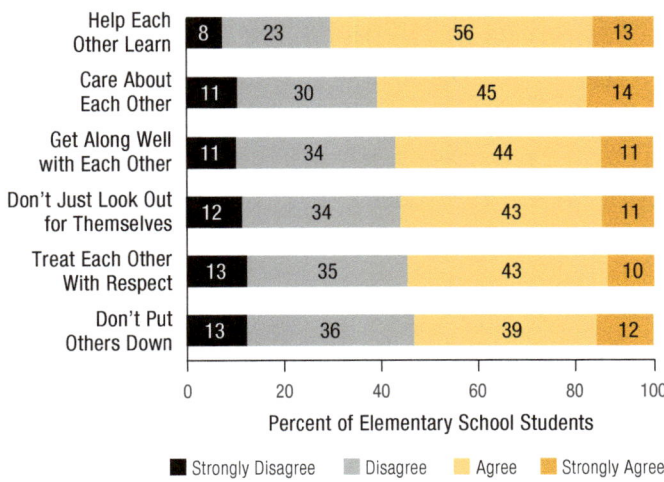
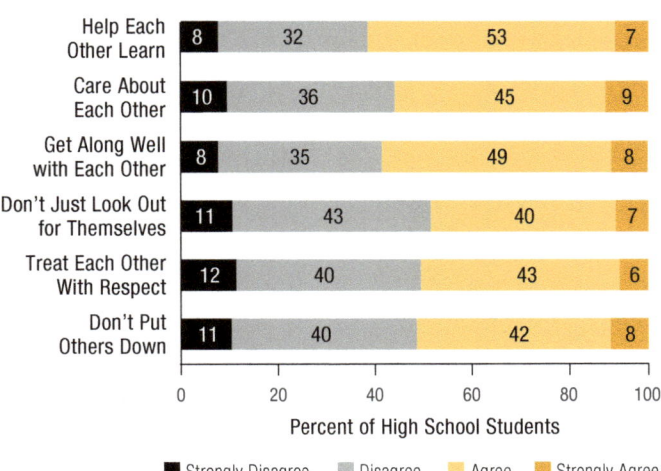

Note: See Appendix A for details about the sample of teacher and student respondents and response rates, and about the representativeness of the survey responses for all CPS students and teachers. Of the six item responses associated with *Student Perceptions of Peer Interactions*, the language of the following four items was changed to make the wording of all item responses parallel: "Don't really care about each other" to "Care about each other"; "Don't get along together very well" to "Get along well with each other"; "Just look out for themselves" to "Don't just look out for themselves"; and "Like to put others down" to "Don't put others down."

traveling to and from school. Thus, large numbers of students feel at least some concern for their safety on the way to school and back, and especially when they are close to the school building.

It might seem surprising that the area just outside of the school holds the most concern for students, rather than areas that are more distant from the school itself. However, consider the environmental constraints that students face when coming to, or leaving, the school. Students have some choice in determining their routes to and from school and may be able to avoid situations and areas they deem less safe. However, there is no choice about entering the area around the school. It is difficult to avoid others with whom a student may have a conflict, and the aggregation of large numbers of students with little adult supervision in a confined area may result in tensions among students. Furthermore, some students may be accompanied by adults or older siblings as they travel to school, until they reach the outside of the school building. In general, student safety appears related to the level of adult supervision, as students feel least safe in areas outside of the school, more safe in common areas such as hallways and bathrooms where there may be some supervision, and most safe in their classrooms where there is a teacher present.

The influence of adult supervision on students' feelings of safety can also be seen in the way that students rate interactions among their peers (see Figure 3). Among both elementary and high school students, there are large numbers of students who report low levels of respect and care among peers; only about half of students report that students at their school treat each other with respect, and half say that students at their school just look out for themselves. Half of all students report that their peers tend to "put others down." However, the majority of students say that students at their school help each other learn. Interviews with eighth- and ninth-graders have shown that the place that students help each other learn is predominantly in the classroom, not outside of the school building or even after school.[35] As it does with student perceptions of school safety, the presence of adults appears to mitigate adverse social interactions.

Crime and Disorder Is a Serious Concern for Most CPS High School Teachers and Many Elementary School Teachers

Prior CCSR research has shown that the school factor that is most strongly predictive of whether or not high school teachers continue teaching in their school is the degree to which it is a safe environment.[36] Teachers do not want to stay where they do not feel the climate is conducive for them to be effective. For about one-third of CPS high school teachers, disrespect and hallway disorder are serious problems; an additional one-third of high school teachers are at least somewhat concerned with these issues (see Figure 4). More than half of high school teachers report problems associated with robbery or theft in their school, and more than 60 percent report significant problems with gang activity and physical conflicts among students. More than one-quarter of high school teachers report significant student threats of violence toward teachers in their school. Given the substantial issues with crime and disorder faced by many high school teachers, it is not surprising that this element so strongly defines whether they stay or leave their school.

Elementary and middle school (K–8) teachers report fewer problems than their high school counterparts, but crime and disorder are still troublesome problems for many. Nearly half of K–8 teachers report problems related to disorder in the classrooms and hallways, physical conflicts among students, and student disrespect of teachers. One-third of K–8 teachers report that gang activity is a problem. Only half of K–8 teachers say that there are no problems with violent threats towards teachers.

In general, there is a strong correspondence between student and teacher reports of safety; no school is reported to be very safe or very unsafe by one group and not by the other (see Figure 1). The fact that two different groups of respondents with different survey questions produce similar reports about school climate provides additional validation that the surveys capture real differences in school safety, even though they are based on self-reports. Thus, when we identify schools that are generally unsafe, both teachers and students tend to report concerns.

There Have Been Some Improvements in Elementary/Middle School Safety Since 2007

Taken as a whole, the student and teacher survey responses in 2009 present a picture of concern regarding school safety for many students and teachers. However, from 2007 to 2009 there were some improvements in teachers' reports of crime and disorder at the K–8 level, and also in middle school students' reports of respectful peer interactions (see Tables 2 and 3). These improvements are significant, even taking into account any changes in student body composition that may have occurred across the two years. Unfortunately, safety did not improve between 2007 and 2009 at the high school level, where the largest problems exist.[37]

FIGURE 4

Teacher reports of crime and disorder in their school

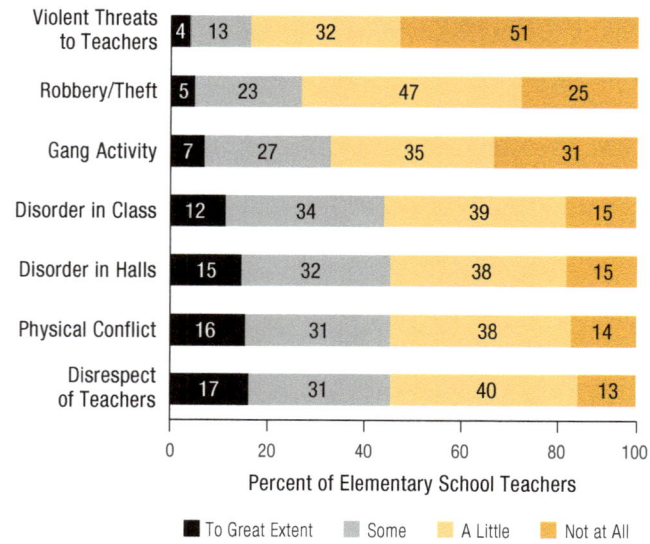
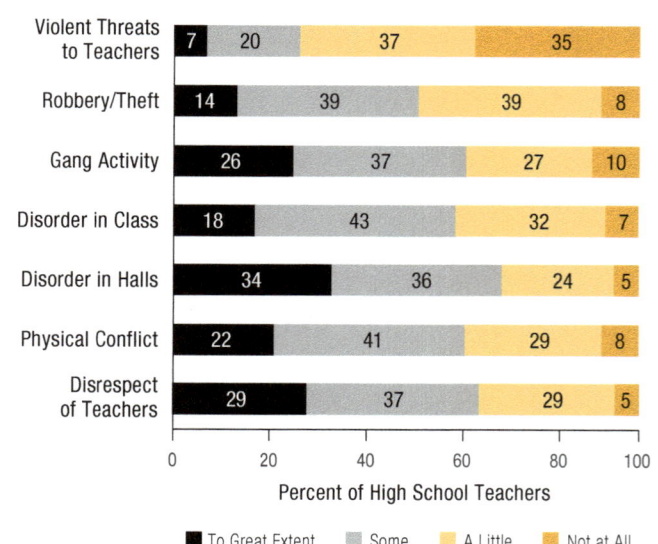

Note: See Appendix A for details about the sample of teacher and student respondents and response rates, and about the representativeness of the survey responses for all CPS students and teachers

TABLE 2

Responses from elementary school students on peer interactions, 2007–09

Most Students in My School...	Agree or Strongly Agree	
	2007	2009
Help Others Learn	65%	69%
Care About Others	55%	59%
Get Along Well	51%	55%
Look Out for Others	51%	54%
Treat Others Respectfully	47%	53%
Don't Put Others Down	46%	51%

Note: Item responses for student i are weighted as the inverse of school j's response rate on the student survey in year t (e.g., $Weight_{it} = 1/ResponseRate_{jt}$). These figures are based on all schools that participated in each of the surveys; similar improvements are observed if we limit the comparison to those schools that participated in both survey years.

TABLE 3

Responses from elementary school teachers, 2007–09

To What Extent Is Each of These a Problem at Your School:	Some or a Lot	
	2007	2009
Violent Threats to Teachers	23%	17%
Robbery/Theft	32%	28%
Gang Activity	36%	34%
Disorder in Class	50%	46%
Disorder in Hallways	52%	47%
Physical Conflict	55%	48%
Disrespect of Teachers	54%	47%

Note: Item responses for teacher i are weighted as the inverse of school j's response rate on the teacher survey in year t (e.g., $Weight_{it} = 1/ResponseRate_{jt}$).

Chapter 2

Safety by Type of School and Neighborhood

Safety is a particularly pressing issue in urban public schools, in part because community factors such as crime and poverty play a strong role in shaping the climate of schools. A number of studies have shown that neighborhood characteristics, including crime and poverty, influence the social and educational development of children and the climate of schools.[38] At the same time, if they are to be successful learners, students living in areas with high levels of poverty and crime may be most in need of a safe schooling environment to mitigate the violence that they experience outside of school.

This chapter shows that neighborhood factors—particularly the extent of crime and poverty in students' home communities—are related to student and teacher feelings of safety in Chicago schools. However, as shown later in this chapter, the influence of neighborhood crime and poverty on school safety operates largely through the clustering of students with high and low academic achievement across schools. It is the gathering together of many students with low academic achievement and weak attachment to school that is most problematic for school safety. However, neighborhood contexts and the clustering of students by achievement level are not the only factors that define safety in schools. It is important to note that there are large differences in safety among schools serving similar types of students, a fact that we explore in greater depth in Chapter 3.

> It is the gathering together of many students with low academic achievement and weak attachment to school that is most problematic for school safety.

Crime and Poverty in Students' Residential Neighborhoods Matter More than Crime and Poverty Around the School

As would be expected, Chicago schools located in areas with higher crime rates and more poverty tend to be less safe. Crime in the neighborhood around the school accounts for a little more than one-quarter of the differences across schools in student and teacher reports of safety and peer interactions, while poverty around the school explains approximately 20 percent of these differences (see Figure 5). However, while the location of the school does matter, the characteristics of students' home neighborhoods are more important. Many students in Chicago travel outside of their neighborhood to attend school; nearly 60 percent of high school students and 50 percent of elementary school students in CPS attend a school other than their neighborhood school. Both crime and poverty in students' home neighborhoods explain approximately one-third of the differences in students' and teachers' feelings of safety, and close to half of the differences across schools in the quality of peer interactions (see Figure 5). Thus, school safety is strongly defined by the characteristics of a school's student population—who attends the school and the neighborhoods in which they live. Peer interactions, in particular, are less supportive and respectful in schools with greater percentages of students from high-poverty, high-crime neighborhoods.

Schools Are Safer when Students Come from Communities with More Social Resources

Neighborhood poverty and crime may contribute to school safety through a number of mechanisms, one of which is the degree to which neighbors provide support to each other and watch over children in the community. Other research has found that neighborhood collective efficacy—the extent of social cohesion among neighbors coupled with neighbors' willingness to intervene on behalf of the common good—is particularly related to neighborhood violence and victimization.[39] Correspondingly, we find that school safety is better the more that students in the school report that there

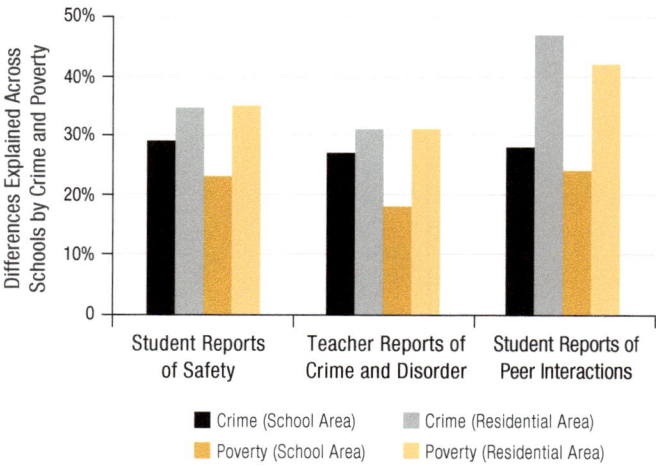

FIGURE 5

School safety is more strongly related to poverty and crime in students' residential neighborhoods than to poverty and crime in the area around the school

Note: Each bar represents the percent of variation explained (R^2) from a regression of each of the three survey measures on school or student-area crime or poverty (n = 541 for student reports and 432 for teacher reports). School-area characteristics (crime, poverty) are based on the census block group where the school is located. Residential-area characteristics are based on the weighted average of the census block groups in which the students in the school live. The crime measure is based on Chicago Police Department incident statistics during the January to June 2009 period, and is calculated as the log (crime rate), where the crime rate is the ratio of total number of crimes to the total population by census block. The measure of poverty is a composite mean, at the census block level, based on the percent of males over 18 years old employed for one or more weeks during the year and the percent of families living above the poverty line (the measure is reverse coded so that higher values indicate greater levels of concentrated poverty). The measure of social status is a composite mean, at the census block level, based on the percent of employed persons 16 years or older who are managers or executives and the mean level of education of persons over age 18.

are human and social resources in their home neighborhoods.[40] In fact, human and social resources in the community play as important a role in explaining students' perceptions of school safety as do crime and poverty in a student's home neighborhood (see Row 5, Table 4, compared to Rows 1–4). Students feel safer coming and going to school, around the school, and in the school building if they come from communities where adults know the neighborhood children and work together to keep the community safe. Human and social resources in the community are much less strongly associated with teachers' feelings of safety than with students' feelings of safety, although they are also related. This makes sense, as it is students who would be receiving support from adults in the community rather than teachers.

One might also expect the presence of more affluent families in some communities, where residents have more education and more are employed in managerial, professional, or executive jobs, to be associated with fewer safety concerns. However, only modest relationships exist, regardless of whether they are measured in the area around the school or in students' home neighborhoods (see Rows 6–7, Table 4), and they are completely attributable to the fact that neighborhoods with more affluent families also have less poverty and lower crime rates. It is the presence or absence of poverty and crime, more than the presence of higher-income families, that correlates with school safety.

The Nature and Severity of Safety Issues Change when Students Enter High School

As shown in Chapter 1, school safety is somewhat better in elementary schools than in high schools. In particular, high school teachers are more likely to report that gang activity is a substantial problem—over one-quarter view it as a great problem, while two-thirds say gang activity is somewhat of a problem. High school teachers are also much more likely than elementary teachers to report substantial problems with disorder in the hallways and disrespect of teachers. Interviews with students from the qualitative sample reflect the differences perceived in the teacher surveys. Students report that the nature of their encounters with gang activity changes as they move to high school so that it becomes a more direct threat. Furthermore, students are less likely to personally know staff members and other students in high school than in elementary/middle school; this can result in misunderstandings among people who do not know each other well, which can lead to conflict. Schools' disciplinary strategies are also a greater concern for students when they move into ninth grade. These differences are described further

TABLE 4

Relationships of school safety with community and school context

		Student Reports of Safety Grades six to 12	Teacher Reports of Crime and Disorder Grades K–12	Student Reports of Peer Interactions Grades six to 12
Community Context	1. Crime in School Neighborhood	-0.54	-0.52	-0.54
	2. Crime in Students' Home Neighborhoods	-0.60	-0.57	-0.69
	3. Poverty in School Neighborhood	-0.50	-0.46	-0.51
	4. Poverty in Students' Home Neighborhoods	-0.60	-0.57	-0.66
	5. Human and Social Resources in Students' Home Neighborhoods	0.60	0.44	0.53
	6. Higher Status Families in the School Neighborhood	0.37	0.20	0.19
	7. Higher Status Families in Students' Home Neighborhoods	0.38	0.23	0.14
School Structure	8. School Level (High School vs. Elementary School)	-0.34	-0.28	-0.14
	9. Enrollment Size	-0.05	-0.07	0.10
School Composition	10. Percent Low-Income	-0.66	-0.49	-0.52
	11. Math and Reading Achievement of Students Entering Ninth Grade (High Schools) or Sixth Grade (Elementary/Middle)	0.69	0.72	0.70
	12. Percent African American	-0.49	-0.51	-0.70
	13. Percent Latino	0.22	0.30	0.48
	14. Percent White	0.66	0.52	0.58
	15. Percent Asian	0.33	0.31	0.40

Note: Relationships indicated are bivariate correlations, where 0 = no relationship and 1 or -1 indicate perfect positive or negative relationships, respectively. Stronger relationships are indicated with darker colors. N = 524 schools for student reports of safety and interactions and 388 schools for teacher reports. All correlations are significant at p<.001 except enrollment size.

in the sidebar "Students' Perceptions of Issues around Safety as They Move into High School."

Yet, while there are marked differences in safety between middle grades and high school grades, these differences are overshadowed by the differences in safety by community context. The relationship between grade level and school safety is about half of the size of the relationship between safety and community context factors, and there is only a very modest relationship between grade level and the quality of student interactions (see Row 8, Table 4). While the schools with the worst safety in the city are all high schools, other high schools are among the safest schools in the city (see Figure 1), and many K–8 schools struggle with issues of safety and order. Safety at the school is much more strongly determined by where the school is located, and the backgrounds of the students at the school, than by the grade levels it serves. For this reason, many of the students interviewed for the Focus on Freshmen study (see the sidebar "Students' Perceptions of Issues around Safety as They Move into High School") did not find high school to be dramatically different in terms of safety than their elementary school. Even if they were attending high school at one of the least safe schools in the district, they did not necessarily view the environment as much less safe than their elementary school because their elementary school was also a place where few students or teachers felt safe.

School Safety Is Unrelated to School Size

School size––the number of students enrolled in the school—is also not a strong determinant of either students' or teachers' perceptions of safety (see Row 9, Table 4). Even if we look at particular sizes of schools (e.g., very small, small, medium, large, very large), at either the K–8 or high school level, there are no systematic differences. Some of the least safe schools are large, but some of the safest schools are also very large. Some of the safest schools are small, as well as some of the most unsafe schools.

Schools Serving African American Students Are the Least Safe, Particularly in the Quality of Interactions Among Students

There are large differences in school safety across schools with different racial compositions of students. Students attending schools that serve predominantly African American students feel much less safe and report less positive peer interactions than students at other schools, on average. Teachers at these schools also report substantially less safe environments (see Figure 6). The biggest difference in safety between African American schools and others is in the quality of peer interactions, with African American students especially unlikely to say their peers treat each other with respect. The schools that are most safe, on all three aspects of safety, are those that are majority

FIGURE 6

African American schools tend to have the lowest levels of safety

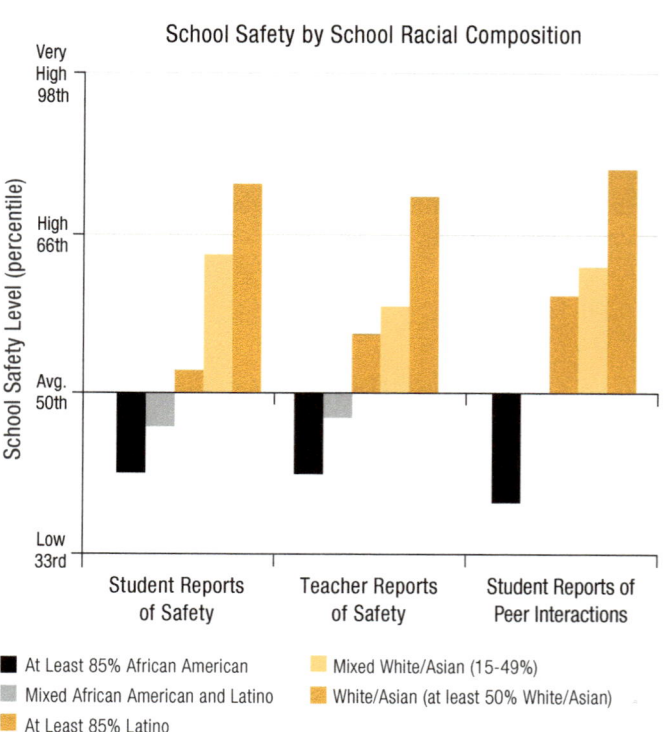

Note: Each line on the graph represents half of an effect size. The difference between "Average" and "High" is one standard deviation. A school's racial composition falls under one of five mutually exclusive categories. For student reports, the chart is based on 250 African American schools, 91 mixed African American and Latino schools (at least 85 percent African American and Latino), 78 Latino schools, 79 schools between 15 and 49 percent white or Asian, and 45 schools majority white or Asian schools. For teacher reports, there are 189 African American schools, 81 mixed African American and Latino schools, 71 Latino schools, 64 schools with between 15 and 49 white or Asian, and 36 majority white or Asian schools. The F-statistic from a test of equality of means indicates that the mean level of each of the three safety measures is significantly different by school racial composition.

Students' Perceptions of Issues around Safety as They Move into High School

To study the transition to high school, we interviewed students as they moved from eighth grade to ninth grade in five neighborhood high schools.[41] The climate of safety in these high schools ranges from somewhat above average at one school to far below average. In all of these schools there are some students who feel safe and others who do not, depending on many factors other than the overall school climate. These include the students' personal characteristics, whether they have friends or family members at the school that they can depend on to help them, the types of peers with whom they associate, and their feelings about adults in the building. Among those students who have serious concerns, many feel less safe in high school than in their K–8 middle school. The overriding concerns in both elementary and high school are around gangs and fighting, but the nature of those problems changes when students enter high school.

Gang Activity Becomes More Directly Threatening

During the transition to high school, gang problems become more directly present in many students' everyday lives. Students are aware of gangs, gang graffiti, shootings, and even gang-affiliated peers in eighth grade, but their concerns seem to be mostly external to the school—in the neighborhood outside the school, or in their home neighborhoods. In high school, gang issues are present inside the school building and increasingly involve students' friends and acquaintances. Students are more likely to face issues of recruitment into gangs and accidental involvement with gang activity. They become careful about choosing their associates and are particularly worried about being mistaken for gang members themselves. This was less of a concern when they were younger and affiliated with younger peers. *"You have to watch what you're saying—have to watch who you talk to,"* a high school student explains.

Fighting Leads to Course Absences

The character of fighting also changes across the transition to high school. Students observe that fights in high school are larger, less controlled, and more dangerous. The one-on-one scuffling of elementary school gives way to groups of students engaged in what occasionally become wild, melee-style brawls. As one student notes, kids at high school *"would rather jump [in a group] than go one-on-one."* Conflicts also grow out of control more quickly in high school. Another student described how rapidly the transition from fight to brawl can occur:

> There was a fight . . . and everybody surrounded [them], and [then], everybody just started hitting everybody . . . and I was like, 'Oh my God, how am I going to get through this to get to class?!'

Heightened fears about threats and fighting make students more likely to avoid school in ninth grade. In eighth grade, none of the students we interviewed said they stayed away from school because of safety concerns; however, ninth-grade students sometimes reported staying home or leaving school early to avoid trouble:

> They were gonna have a big war in front of the school . . . but that day I called my mom and I told her to pick me up early, so just in case anything happened I won't be in the middle. So she came and got me early.

Anonymity and Weak Relationships Make Conflict More Likely

The greater anonymity of the high school—fostered by its size, the mixing of students from dozens of elementary feeder schools, and the decrease in sustained contact between children and adults—makes it more difficult to prevent conflicts from occurring in the first place. In eighth grade, teachers were dealing with smaller numbers of students, sometimes in self-contained classrooms, and were more aware of, and responsive to, emerging conflicts. Elementary school teachers were able to take students aside, draw on students' relationships to other adults in the building, and involve administrators and parents more constructively to resolve conflict before it became violent. Elementary school teachers also devoted more time to group dynamics in their classes, sometimes holding whole-class meetings to discuss and learn from disagreements and fights. In high schools, adults are less likely to know all of the parties involved in a conflict, or to be aware of emerging conflicts. This limits their opportunities to be proactive in curtailing disagreements before they become violent. Absent the deeper relationships with students and families more characteristic of elementary school teachers, adults at the high school level take a less active role in anticipating and preventing conflicts.

There is also a greater chance for misunderstanding among students and between students and teachers who know each other only superficially.

> "It's easier to get in trouble in [high school]," a student explains. "It's more people, so it's easy to either get picked on or somebody throw something at somebody—and you can come to the wrong person and [then] it's a fight. In [elementary school] you know who did it, 'cause there's only like 20 people in the class and you know them."

Discipline Becomes Harsher

Disciplinary measures in high school become more severe as teachers react to, rather than preempt, conflict. With the exception of one elementary school in the study with frequent suspensions, conflicts among eighth-grade students were often likely to be resolved through conversations. Students would be sent to sit with the principal, talk with a staff member, or resolve a conflict with the teacher. In the larger, more anonymous environment of the high school, conflicts and fights often resulted in out-of-school suspensions. Ninth-graders are surprised both by the severity of punishments their peers receive and by the stricter enforcement of school rules.

More Effective Security and Police Presence Can Ease Concerns

Many students appreciate the more overt presence of security guards and police in high schools and say it makes them feel safer. Some contrast security measures in high school with those of their elementary school, where they felt it unlikely that hall monitors would intervene in a serious fight. When asked whether she felt safe in her high school, a student explained that she did: "... 'cause around here you see cops around the school, and security guards, so it makes you feel good. In [middle school] there was a security guard, but not like police out here, over there."

However, students see security as more effective in some schools than in others. In one high school, students felt that security guards did not intervene effectively to prevent or stop fights; instead they became involved to punish students after the fact. In another high school, security guards were active in hallways, but students felt verbally and physically harassed. Security guards sometimes seemed to exacerbate conflicts by aggressively restraining students; instead of resolving conflicts, these security guards seemed to become part of the conflicts themselves. As one student observed, *"towards the teachers, and some [students] they know,"* security guards at this high school *"act normal. But then once [security] get[s] to . . . other people, they want to fight, cuss, and argue."* As with teachers, the most functional security guards seemed to have relationships with students that made them more aware of, and receptive to, resolving conflicts proactively before they became violent.

White/Asian. Schools that are predominantly Latino fall in-between, but not in a systematic way across all three indicators of safety. While Latino schools tend to have more positive, respectful interactions among students than the average CPS school, students' feelings of safety in and around the school are only at the district average.

It is difficult to disentangle school racial composition from neighborhood characteristics like crime and poverty. Almost all schools serving students from neighborhoods with the highest levels of crime and poverty are African American schools (see Figure 7). Most schools with a substantial proportion of White or Asian students serve students from neighborhoods with low or very low crime rates. Predominantly Latino schools serve students from neighborhoods with average levels of crime. There is very little overlap in the social/economic conditions of students' neighborhoods when we consider schools that are predominantly of one racial-ethnic group. Therefore, while the most unsafe schools in the district are all African American schools and the safest schools contain a majority White and Asian student population, these schools serve students from the highest- and lowest-crime neighborhoods, respectively.[42]

The School Feature Most Strongly Associated with Safety Is the Entering Academic Achievement Level of Its Students

While school safety is strongly related to students' neighborhood characteristics, it is even more strongly related to the academic skills of students served by the school—the average achievement levels of students who enter the middle grades or high school (see Table 4 on page 23).[43] On average, students in Chicago who attend schools that enroll higher-achieving students report feeling safer at school than students in schools serving students with lower academic skills. In fact, school achievement level explains approximately *half* of the differences in student reports of overall safety and teacher reports of crime and disorder and the differences in the quality of interactions among peers at both the elementary and high school levels.

FIGURE 7

School safety is related to racial composition because racial composition is related to neighborhood crime and poverty

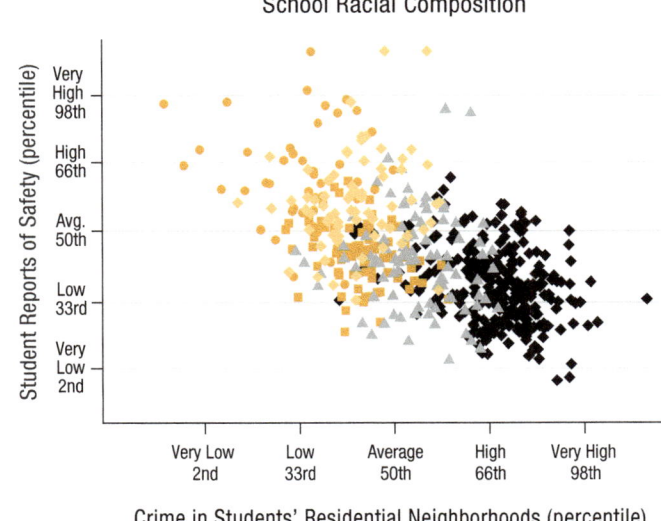

◆ At Least 85% African American ◆ Mixed White/Asian (15-49%)
▲ Mixed African American and Latino ● White/Asian (at least 50% White/Asian)
■ At Least 85% Latino

Note: Each dot represents a single school. Safer schools are in the upper portion of the chart, and unsafe schools are in the bottom portion of the chart. "Very Low" represents two standard deviations below the mean. "Low" represents one standard deviation below the mean. "Average" is the mean. "High" is one standard deviation above the mean. "Very High" is two standard deviations above the mean. For *Student Reports of Safety*, data is available for 250 schools that are at least 85 percent African American, 91 schools that are mixed African American and Latino (e.g., at least 85 percent African American and Latino students), 78 schools that are at least 85 percent Latino, 79 schools that are mixed with between 15 and 49 percent of students either White or Asian, and 45 schools that are a majority White or Asian (e.g., at least 50 percent of students are either White or Asian).

The magnitude of the relationship of achievement to student perceptions of safety is similar across elementary and high school students, using different measures of achievement (fifth-grade ISAT scores in the elementary schools and ninth-grade entering EXPLORE scores in the high schools). One interpretation of this relationship may be that achievement is higher because safety is higher—that students are better able to concentrate on learning when they are in a safe environment. This is likely true, and other research has shown that schools are more likely to show improvements in test scores if they have safe learning climates.[44] However, in this case, school achievement level is measured with students' *incoming* test scores at the beginning of ninth grade (for high school reports) or the end of fifth grade (for students in grades six through eight). Thus, it is the characteristics of students that show a relationship with safety, not the quality of the education they received while at the high school or in the middle grades.[45]

Not only is school average incoming achievement level the strongest predictor of student reports of school safety, but it also explains most of the relationship of school safety with poverty and crime. Alone, poverty and crime are strongly related to students' reports of school safety. But after accounting for student reports of human and social resources in the community and the achievement level of the school, crime and poverty show only a modest relationship with student safety in elementary schools and no relationship in high schools (see Figure 8). Poverty and crime show strong relationships with school safety primarily because schools in high-poverty, high-crime areas tend to have low achievement. Student achievement levels also explain most of the relationship of crime and poverty with teacher perceptions of crime and disorder in the school. The relationship between crime and poverty and teacher reports of safety shrinks to about one-third of its original size in elementary schools and becomes almost non-existent in high schools once we account for the achievement level of the school and the extent of human and social resources in the student's home communities. Student achievement level does not completely explain the relationship that poverty and crime have with the quality of peer interactions, although it does explain part of it; shrinking to two-thirds of its original size for elementary schools and about half for high schools.

Safety Differs Substantially Among Schools Serving Similar Students

Figures 9–11 provide more detail on the strong relationships between school safety and the characteristics of students attending the school—the degree to which they live in neighborhoods with poverty and crime, and their academic achievement levels. There is almost no overlap in student reports of safety among schools serving students with the most disadvantaged backgrounds and schools serving the most advantaged students. Safety in the school is strongly defined by the characteristics of the students served by the school.

At the same time, student characteristics are *not* completely deterministic of the level of safety of the school. There are very large differences in safety among schools serving similar types of students. Schools

FIGURE 8

The relationship of neighborhood crime and poverty with school safety is mostly attributable to school achievement level and human/social resources in the community

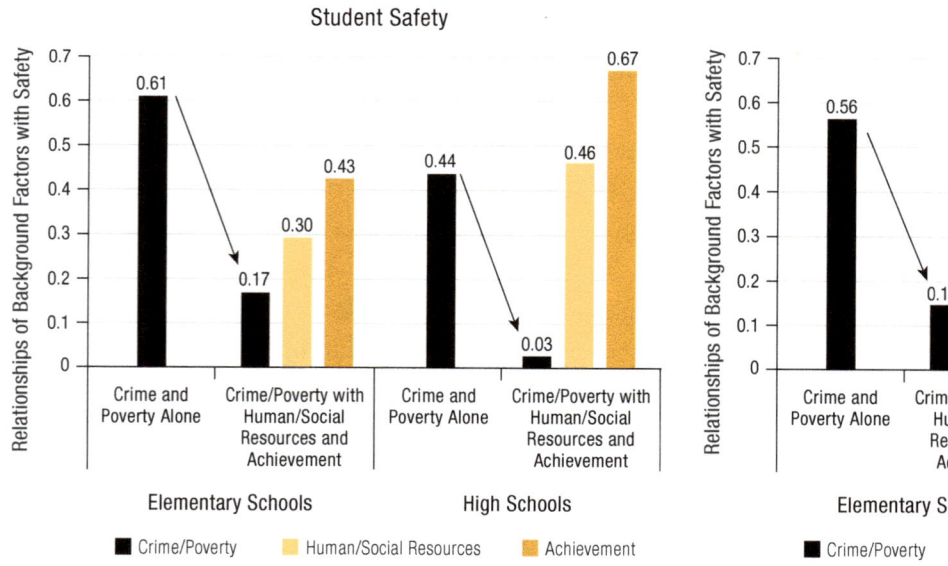
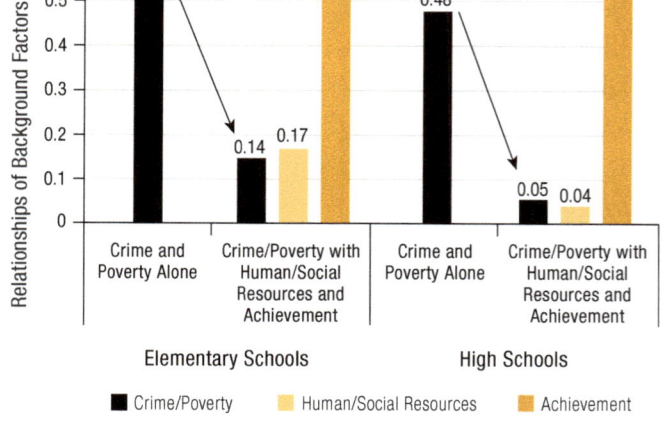

Note: For purposes of display, crime and poverty are combined into one factor where higher values on crime and poverty represent less crime and poverty; this makes the relationship with safety positive. Each bar represents a standardized coefficient from a regression of student or teacher safety on crime and poverty (combined into one indicator), with human/social resources and school achievement included in a second model. Crime/poverty is a composite of student residential area crime and poverty, and human/social resources is the standardized value of the student survey measure Human and Social Resources in the Community. For elementary schools, achievement is the standardized proportion of students in grades six to eight in the 2008–09 school year who met or exceeded proficiency on the reading and math portions of the ISAT when they were in fifth grade. For high schools, achievement is the standardized mean EXPLORE reading and math score results for ninth-grade students administered in the fall of the 2008–09 school year.

Pacific, Huron, and Lake Erie: Typical Levels of Safety for the Students They Serve

Not surprisingly, Lake Erie school, which struggles with high levels of crime and disorder, and non-respectful interactions among students, also serves a very disadvantaged student population (see Table B). Its students come from neighborhoods with high rates of crime and poverty; over one-third of the families in students' home neighborhoods live below the poverty line, and male unemployment is at 50 percent. Students also enter Lake Erie with extremely low levels of achievement—their average incoming test scores are in the bottom 10 percent of all CPS high schools. Huron serves students that are average for CPS, in terms of crime and poverty in the neighborhoods from which they come, and in terms of their entering test scores. At Pacific, students come from neighborhoods that are similar to Huron in terms of crime and poverty. However, Pacific enrolls very high-achieving students. As noted earlier, student achievement level is the strongest contextual factor related to safety. Thus, although Pacific students do not come from advantaged neighborhoods, the school is safe and orderly.

TABLE B

Characteristics of case study high schools

Community Context	Pacific A Safe High School	Huron A Typical High School	Lake Erie An Unsafe High School
Crime in Students' Neighborhoods	Average Crime	Average Crime	High Crime
Poverty Rate in Students' Neighborhoods	18.0%	24.7%	37.6%
Male Unemployment in Students' Neighborhoods	37.8%	28.8%	50.4%
School Context	**Pacific** A Safe High School	**Huron** A Typical High School	**Lake Erie** An Unsafe High School
Racial Composition	Mixed African American and Latino	Predominantly Latino	Predominantly African American
Incoming Math Achievement	Very High Achieving	Average Achieving	Very Low Achieving
Incoming Reading Achievement	Very High Achieving	Average Achieving	Very Low Achieving

Note: The Poverty Rate is the percentage of families living below the poverty level, based on the neighborhoods in which the students live. Male Unemployment is the percentage of men 16 years of age and older who did not work in 1999, based on the neighborhoods in which the students live. Incoming Math Achievement and Incoming Reading Achievement consist of the mean EXPLORE math and reading scores for ninth-grade students administered in the fall of the 2008–09 school year. For Pacific, the crime rate (e.g., the average number of crimes per 100 residents) in the students' home neighborhoods is 6.6; for Huron, the crime rate is 5.3; and for Lake Erie, the crime rate is 10.9.

serving students from neighborhoods with the highest crime rates range from some of the very least safe in the system to others at about the 66th percentile (see Figure 9). Likewise, there are schools that serve students from very low-crime neighborhoods that are less safe than the average CPS school, despite serving more advantaged students. Schools serving students from neighborhoods with average levels of crime vary quite dramatically in how students report safety in their schools. Some are among the safest schools in CPS (at the 99th percentile), while other schools serving students from neighborhoods with identical levels of crime are among the least safe (at the 10th percentile). Similar patterns of large differences in teacher reports of safety and student reports of peer interactions can be seen among schools serving students from neighborhoods with similar crime rates, poverty levels, and achievement, although those figures are not shown in this report. The differences are also not attributable to measurement error, as described in Appendix C.

Thus, schools serving students with very similar circumstances can have very different levels of safety. That is, *demographics are not destiny when it comes to school safety*. In the next section, we examine the reasons these differences exist. We explore the ways schools are organized in terms of the manner in which people in the school work together—the social-organizational structure—to identify the mechanisms through which some schools produce safe schooling environments while others do not.

FIGURE 9
Student reports of school safety by crime in their residential neighborhoods

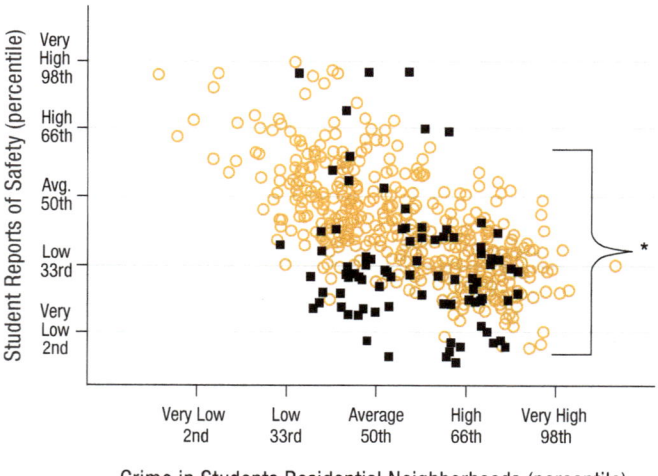

○ Elementary School ■ High School

* There are large differences in safety even among schools serving the highest-crime neighborhoods

Note: Each dot represents one school (543 total schools; 452 elementary and 91 high schools). The correlation coefficient = -.59. We make double adjustments for measurement error, as described in Appendix C. "Very Low" is two standard deviations below the mean; in these communities, the crime rate is about two per 100 residents. "Low" is one standard deviation below the mean; in these communities, the crime rate is about four per 100 residents. "Average" is the mean; in these communities, the crime rate is about six per 100 residents. "High" is one standard deviation above the mean; in these communities, the crime rate is about 10 per 100 residents. "Very High" is two standard deviations above the mean; in these communities, the crime rate is about 16 per 100 residents.

FIGURE 10
Student reports of school safety by poverty in their residential neighborhoods

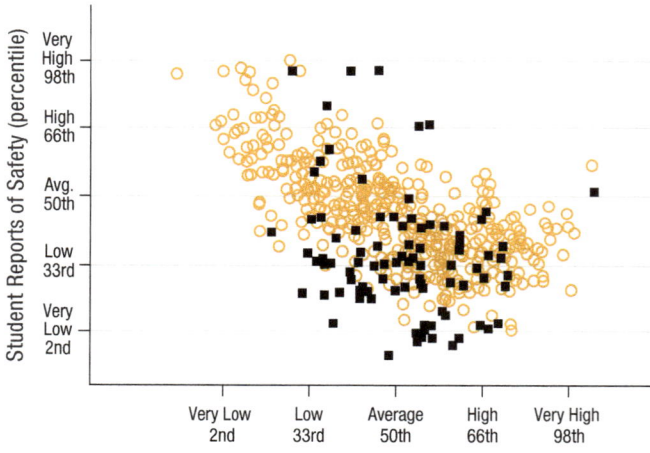

○ Elementary School ■ High School

Note: Each dot represents one school (543 total schools; 452 elementary and 91 high schools). The correlation coefficient = -.60. We make double adjustments for measurement error—first, at the student level and again at the school level as described in Appendix C. "Very Low" is two standard deviations below the mean; in these communities (according to the 2000 U.S. Census) 4.5 percent of families live below the poverty level and 21.5 percent of men 16 years and older did not work in 1999. "Low" is one standard deviation below the mean; in these communities 11.7 percent of families live below the poverty level, and 26.4 percent of men 16 years and older did not work in 1999. "Average" is at the mean; in these communities 24.4 percent of families live below the poverty level, and 31.3 percent of men 16 years and older did not work in 1999. "High" is one standard deviation above the mean; in these communities 31.7 percent of families live below the poverty level and 46.9 percent of men 16 years and older did not work in 1999. "Very High" is two standard deviations above the mean; in these communities 53.3 percent of families live below the poverty level, and 53.9 percent of men 16 years and older did not work in 1999.

FIGURE 11

Student reports of school safety by school achievement

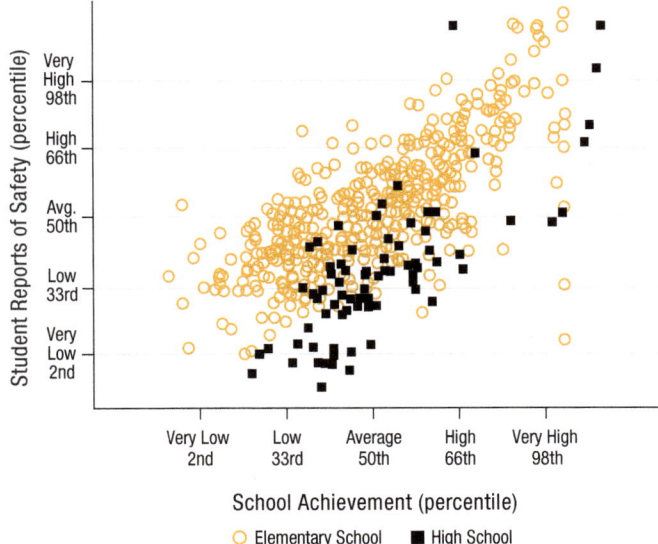

Note: Each dot represents one school (530 total schools; 453 elementary and 77 high schools). The correlation coefficient = .69. We make double adjustments for measurement error—first, at the student level and again at the school level as described in Appendix C. School achievement for elementary schools is the standardized proportion of students in grades six to eight in the 2008–09 school year who met or exceeded proficiency on the ISAT when they were in fifth grade. For high schools, school achievement is the standardized mean EXPLORE reading and math score results for ninth-grade students administered in the fall of the 2008–09 school year. "Very Low" is two standard deviations below the mean; in these elementary schools, approximately 28 percent of sixth- to eighth-grade students were proficient in math and 23 percent in reading when they were in fifth grade. In these high schools, the mean 2008–09 EXPLORE math score is 9.9 and the reading score is 10.4. "Low" is one standard deviation below the mean; in these elementary schools, approximately 43 percent of students were proficient in math and 35 percent in reading. In these high schools, the mean EXPLORE math score is 10.9 and the reading score is 11.2. "Average" is the mean; in these elementary schools, approximately 66 percent of students were proficient in math and 49 percent in reading. In these high schools, the mean EXPLORE math score is 13.3 and the reading score is 12.5. "High" is one standard deviation above the mean; in these elementary schools, approximately 81 percent of students were proficient in math and 70 percent in reading. In these high schools, the mean EXPLORE math score is 15.1 and the reading score is 14.5. "Very High" is two standard deviations above the mean; in these elementary schools, approximately 95 percent of students were proficient in math and 93 percent in reading. In these high schools, the mean EXPLORE math score is 16.8 and the reading score is 16.4.

Chapter 3

Safety by Internal School Organization and Practices

Chapter 2 showed that factors beyond the control of schools—such as neighborhood crime, poverty, and the incoming academic achievement of students—influence the climate of safety at schools. Yet it also showed large differences in safety among schools serving similar students, suggesting that factors under the control of schools may strongly influence school safety. This chapter explores what some of those factors might be and provides a starting point for thinking about how schools can foster safer environments, regardless of the characteristics of the students who walk through the doors.

Specifically, this chapter shows that schools with harsh discipline policies that result in higher rates of suspensions are, in fact, perceived as less safe by students and teachers. Meanwhile, schools are perceived as more safe the more that people work together and build trusting, collaborative relationships. Indeed, the ways in which members of the school community interact with families, students, and their colleagues explain much of the difference in safety across schools. Moreover, the case studies suggest that the ways in which schools involve parents and strategically work with students may encourage or discourage such relationships.

> The ways in which members of the school community interact with families, students, and their colleagues explain much of the difference in safety across schools.

School Safety Tends to Be Worse in Schools with Higher Suspension Rates

Schools that suspend a larger share of their students are, on average, less safe than others (see Figure 12). Whether reported by students or teachers, the relationship between suspension rates and school safety is similar. There is a dramatic decline in safety that corresponds with increasing suspension rates, up to approximately 15 percent. While safety levels—as reported by students and teachers—continue to decline as suspension rates increase beyond 15 percent, the relationship is less strong; after suspension rates reach about 15 percent, schools look fairly similar in terms of safety.

Schools across CPS serve very different populations of students who arrive at school from different social and economic circumstances. Suspensions are a response to school staff's perceptions of threat and concerns about safety; they reflect which schools struggle the most with these issues. However, at best, the pattern shown in Figure 12 suggests that high rates of suspensions do not sufficiently address the problems that schools face—schools with high rates of suspensions are still less safe than others. In fact, further analysis shows that they are less safe than other schools serving similar types of students, but with lower suspension rates. Comparing schools serving the same types of students from the same neighborhood and community circumstances (i.e., controlling for student achievement, racial composition, poverty, crime, community social resources, and school grade level), those with higher suspension rates are significantly less safe, on average.[46] At worst, this suggests that suspensions themselves may aggravate problems with safety. This perspective is consistent with research by others showing that schools with more severe suspension and "zero tolerance" policies often have higher levels of student fear.[47]

Teachers' Reports About Parent Involvement Are the Strongest Predictor of School Safety

Prior research and theory suggests four broad domains of a school's social-organizational structure that could potentially affect the climate of safety in schools. Each

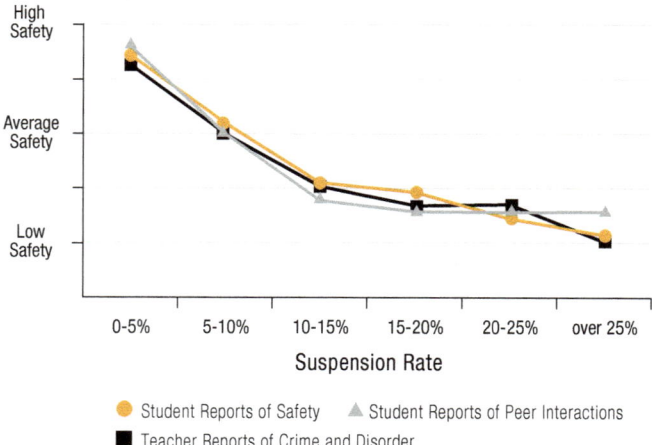

FIGURE 12

Schools with higher suspension rates are less safe, on average

● Student Reports of Safety   ▲ Student Reports of Peer Interactions
■ Teacher Reports of Crime and Disorder

Note: Each node on the graph represents the average level of safety by the percent of students suspended for at least one day during the 2008–09 school year (n = 524 schools for student reports and 388 schools for teacher reports). "High Safety" is one standard deviation above the mean (about the 66th percentile). "Average Safety" is the 50th percentile; and "Low Safety" represents one standard deviation below the mean (about the 33rd percentile). The average suspension rate during the 2008–09 school year was 21.6 percent for high schools and 8.7 percent for K–8 schools.

is examined in this chapter (see Table 5) and described in more detail in Appendix B: (a) school leadership; (b) teacher collaboration and support; (c) school-family interactions; and (d) teacher-student relationships. These domains are defined based on prior CCSR work, which has validated the components in each domain as relevant for school improvement efforts.[48] Each of the organizational features is significantly associated with school safety (see Table 6). What stands out is the degree to which meaningful school-family interactions are particularly important. Both students and teachers feel safest in schools where teachers view parents as partners in children's education. Furthermore, students report more positive peer interactions when they attend schools where teachers report supportive and respectful relationships with students' families. These relationships are stronger than the relationships of neighborhood crime and poverty with safety—and are even stronger than the relationship of safety with school achievement level (see Table 4, Row 11 on page 23).

Collaborative work among teachers also is associated with safer environments, as represented by the relationships between collective responsibility and teacher influence and school safety. The more that teachers take responsibility for the whole school and

Suspensions Can Make Students Feel Unsafe

> Trouble comes along every once in a while. It's bound to happen. Nobody [can] go through a school year without having a suspension or detention.
> —Ninth-grader at Lake Erie

In high schools where student misbehavior is out of control and suspensions are frequent, students can come to perceive suspension as arbitrary and capricious. Suspensions and other forms of discipline seem disconnected from, and out of proportion to, their misdeeds. Being in trouble begins to seem inevitable. As a student noted after being in Lake Erie for a month in ninth grade, *". . . they be suspending people for no reason."* The heavy reliance on punitive disciplinary measures as a means of enforcing safety and order ends up making students feel less in control, less respected and cared for, and, ultimately, less safe.

Students become caught up in trouble, in some cases physically pulled into a fight by crowds of students ringing around and pressing in on a fight as it begins. *"The hallways get crowded,"* a student explains. *"Then you miss your class . . . even if you were trying to run to class, you'll get suspended."* Students' frustration at being suspended for being in the wrong place at the wrong time is palpable.

When students come to view avoiding trouble as beyond their control, it undermines both their sense of fairness and their trust in school staff. In high schools like Lake Erie, students' incentive to comply with the efforts of adults to ensure a safe school environment is undermined, and a cycle of mutual frustration and contempt develops, reinforcing the dynamics that give rise to discipline problems in the first place. An excerpt from observational notes illustrates this cycle:

"Why am I missing so many kids?" the teacher mutters. "Cause you kicked them out," someone says softly. The room is filled with giggles. "When is [student name] coming back?" the teacher asks the class. "Eight more days," someone says. "What about [two other students]?" the teacher continues. "The same," someone else says softly. . . . A school administrator comes to the door. He has three girls who were kicked out of the class earlier lined up in the hallway with their backs against the wall. They had been kicked out after repeatedly interrupting the teacher by singing whenever he would start to speak. Now they are scowling as they stand against the wall. The administrator yells at the girls for what seems like a very long time, ". . . This is your school—would you act a fool like this if you had company at your house?" The girls look at the floor. One girl seems angry; she kicks at the base of the wall forcefully, striking it with the heel of her shoe repeatedly. The administrator concludes by saying that he's "got five days for each of them if they can't get it together." He turns back to the girls and says that they need to have a written apology by the end of the period—and that it needs to be "punctually and grammatically correct." The last thing he says before he leaves the room is that he has "five days if they open their mouth"—he says this to the teacher, but also to the girls; it sounds vindictive and humiliating. Back in the classroom, the girl who was kicking the wall is arguing with some of the other students. One of them is teasing her about having to write an apology. The girl explodes and screams at the other girl—the teacher immediately tells her to leave. By the end of the class, all three students are again thrown out of the classroom by the teacher. They each receive a five-day out-of-school suspension.

TABLE 5
Dimensions and measurement of school social-organizational structure

Domain	CCSR Survey Measure	Description
School Leadership	Teacher Influence (t)	Teacher's involvement in school-based decision making
	Principal Instructional Leadership (t)	Principal's involvement in building/sustaining meaningful instructional environment
	Program Coherence (t)	Extent to which programs in school coordinated with school's goals for instruction and student learning
	Teacher-Principal Trust (t)	Extent of mutual respect between teachers/principals
Teacher Collaboration and Support	Collective Responsibility (t)	Extent of shared commitment among teachers to improve learning
	Orientation to Innovation (t)	Extent of professional development toward improving learning
	Socialization of New Teachers (t)	Extent of feedback on instructional practice/performance
	Teacher-Teacher Trust (t)	Extent teachers trust and respect colleagues
School-Family Interactions	Teacher-Parent Trust (t)	Whether teachers feel that parents act as partners in their students' learning
Student-Teacher Relationships	Teacher Personal Support (s)	Whether students feel their teachers care about their learning and overall well-being
	Student-Teacher Trust (s)	Whether students feel safe with and listened to by their teachers

Note: CCSR survey measures: "t" indicates a teacher survey measure and "s" indicates a student survey measure. Each dimension is measured with a bank of survey questions, which are described in more detail in Appendix B.

TABLE 6
Relationships of school organizational features with school safety

		Student Reports of Safety (n = 524)	Teacher Reports of Safety (n = 387)	Student Reports of Peer Interactions (n = 524)
School Leadership	Teacher Influence (t)	.52	.57	.54
	Principal Instructional Leadership (t)	.20	.34	.21
	Program Coherence (t)	.41	.49	.40
	Teacher-Principal Trust (t)	.28	.38	.29
Teacher Collaboration and Support	Collective Responsibility (t)	.49	.61	.51
	Orientation to Innovation (t)	.43	.51	.45
	Socialization of New Teachers (t)	.38	.42	.42
	Teacher-Teacher Trust (t)	.38	.42	.39
School-Family Interactions	Teacher-Parent Trust (t)	.72	.78	.74
Students' Relationships with Teachers	Teacher Personal Support (s)	.44	.39	.38
	Student-Teacher Trust (s)	.39	.36	.45

Note: Relationships are indicated with bivariate correlations, where 0 = no relationship and 1 or -1 indicate perfect positive or negative relationships, respectively. Stronger relationships are indicated with darker colors. All correlations are significant at p<.001.

work together, rather than just focusing on their individual classrooms, the safer those teachers feel. Likewise, the more that teachers are involved in school decision-making, the safer the environment for both teachers and students. Safety is also higher the more that programs and instruction are coherently coordinated, as indicated by the relationship between safety and program coherence.

School Organization and Practices Explain Differences in Safety Among Schools Serving Similar Students

Table 6 suggests that school relationships and organizational structure matter for school safety; however, it could be that these patterns exist because it is easier to have strong relationships and good organizational structures in schools that serve more advantaged student populations. In other words, it is possible that the relationships themselves do not promote safety; they simply occur naturally in schools already inclined to be safe, based on their student population. However, that is not the case. School relationships and organizational structures explain more of the differences in safety across schools than student and neighborhood context alone (see Figure 13). When we consider the organizational structure of the school (including leadership, teacher collaboration, school-family interactions, and student-teacher relationships), approximately 80 percent of the differences in safety across schools can be explained. Thus, school organizational factors help explain why schools with very similar students can have very different outcomes when it comes to safety.

The importance of fostering strong relationships becomes even more apparent when we consider *why* students from impoverished, high-crime neighborhoods tend to attend less safe schools. Crime and poverty are related to school safety partly *because* schools serving students from more impoverished, high-crime communities are less likely to have strong partnerships between teachers and parents and good relationships between students and teachers. As shown in Figure 14, the relationship between the socioeconomic context in which students live (neighborhood crime, poverty, and the human and social resources in

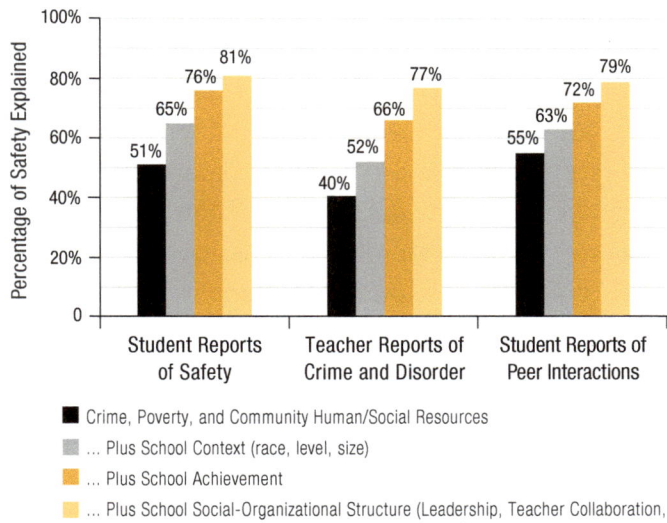

FIGURE 13

School factors explain additional differences in safety beyond neighborhood factors

Note: The percentage of variation explained is the R² from regression models of each of the three safety measures (*Student Reports of Safety*, *Teacher Reports of Crime and Disorder*, and *Student Reports of Peer Interactions*) on the variables listed. For all regressions for *Student Reports of Safety* and *Student Reports of Peer Interactions*, the total number of schools is 524. For all regressions for *Teacher Reports of Crime and Disorder*, the total number of schools is 387. See Table 12 in Appendix D for more details.

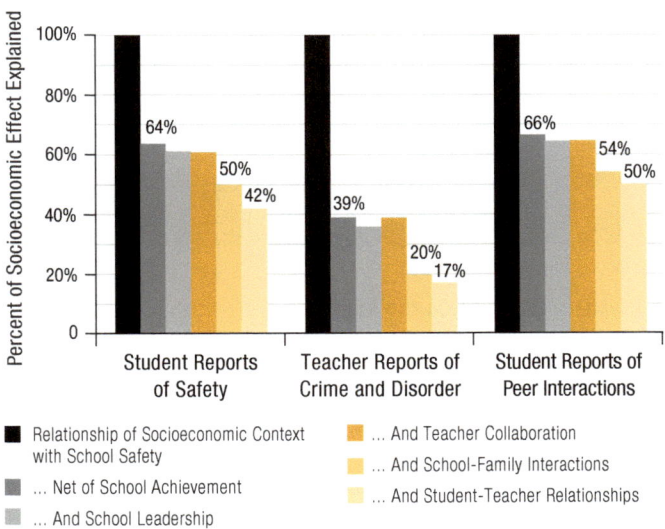

FIGURE 14

School achievement level and social-organizational factors explain why Socioeconomic Context is related to school safety

Note: *Socioeconomic Context* is the total relationship of contextual variables with each indicator of safety, including poverty and crime in the student's home neighborhood and the extent of human and social resources in the student's home community (captured as predicted values from regression equations that modeled safety as an outcome of all contextual variables). The bars represent the size of the coefficient on *Socioeconomic Context* in models that include school features, *relative to* the coefficient from a model with just socioeconomic context. The coefficients are all statistically significant at the 1 percent level. For elementary schools, school achievement is the standardized proportion of students in grades six to eight in the 2008–09 school year who met or exceeded proficiency on the reading and math portions of the ISAT when they were in fifth grade. For high schools, school achievement is the mean EXPLORE reading and math score results for ninth-grade students administered in the fall of the 2008–09 school year.

Chapter 3 | 37

the neighborhood combined) and school safety is much smaller after taking into account teachers' relationships with parents and students. Once we account for social-organizational structure, as well as school achievement level, the relationship between socioeconomic context with students' perceptions of safety is less than half its original size (42 percent). The relationship of peer interactions with socioeconomic context also shrinks to 50 percent of its original size. Moreover, the vast majority of the relationship of socioeconomic context with teachers' perceptions of crime and disorder is explained by the school's internal organization and relationships, along with school achievement level—the relationship is only 17 percent as large once we take into account these other factors. In sum, students' backgrounds strongly affect school safety largely because it is easier to create high-quality relationships in more advantaged school settings.

From Figure 14, it appears that parent-teacher relationships are the most important social-organizational factors influencing school safety. However, the importance of student-teacher relationships is obscured by examining school-family interactions first, since both sets of relationships are related to each other. Table 7 shows the direct relationships that each social-organizational factor has with school safety, net of each of the other social-organizational and school context factors (including neighborhood crime, poverty, and human and social resources and school level, size, and achievement).

When viewed simultaneously, teachers' relationships with students and with parents both are shown to be important for understanding differences in school safety. In fact, the relationships that students have with their teachers are the most important social-organizational factor for students' reports of peer interactions. They are as important as teacher-parent partnerships for students' overall feelings of safety. Teacher-parent trust is still the most important social-organizational structure for teachers' perceptions of crime and disorder in the school, although teachers' relationships with students also matter. Leadership in the school also continues to show a relationship with teachers' reports of crime and safety in the school, after taking into account other social-organizational features, but most of the effects of leadership come through leaders' effects on other mechanisms: the achievement level of students in the school, school-family interactions, and teacher-student relationships. Leadership matters for safety to the extent that it affects these other elements of schools.

TABLE 7

Unique relationships of social-organizational structures on safety, net of all other factors

Variable	Student Perceptions of Safety	Teacher Perceptions of Crime and Disorder	Student Perceptions of Peer Interactions
School Leadership	-0.02	0.08**	-0.01
Teacher Collaboration and Support	0.01	0.03	0.07*
School-Family Interactions *Parent-Teacher Trust*	0.20***	0.35***	0.19***
Student-Teacher Relationships	0.21***	0.16***	0.24***
Number of Schools	524	387	524

Note: Coefficients reported are in standard deviation units. Controls for *Socioeconomic Context* (crime and poverty in the student's home neighborhood and the extent of social resources in the student's home community), school racial composition, school enrollment during the 2008–09 school year, an indicator for whether the school is a high school or elementary school and school achievement were included in the models that produced these coefficients, but not reported in the table. *School Achievement* is a composite of a school's average math and reading achievement. See Table 5 for a list of the CCSR survey measures included in the School Leadership, Teacher Collaboration and Support, School-Family Interactions, and Student-Teacher measures. Coefficients are statistically significant at the *10 percent, **5 percent, and ***1 percent levels.

Case Study

An Uninviting Reception Makes It Difficult for Parents To Be Partners

Schools struggling with violence and safety face a complex challenge: developing and sustaining open and trusting relationships between students and teachers, and between teachers and parents.

The quality of the relationships between students and teachers, and between teachers and parents, reflects a deeply problematic quandary: in high schools like Lake Erie—where students and teachers alike struggle to navigate a chaotic, verbally abusive, and often physically menacing school environment—the difficulty of creating and maintaining mutually respectful and trusting relationships between children, parents, and adults in the school is magnified by constant threats of disrespect and violence. The ways in which schools meet this challenge—by working to foster respectful, trusting relationships within the school environment—can ameliorate or aggravate the effects of low levels of perceived safety.

The structure and tenor of interactions between school staff and parents play an important part in the development of trusting relationships between parents and teachers, and, indirectly, between teachers and students. In unsafe schools like Lake Erie, encounters between parents and school staff are charged by the chaotic, antagonistic environment of the school itself. The main office, where parents and visitors are directed upon entering the school, is frequently noisy and crowded. Interactions between school staff, parents, and visitors are testy and sometimes openly argumentative. At Lake Erie, the main office is covered with signs, many of which are injunctions or instructions to parents: where to sign in; where to wait; expectations for visitors' behavior. Behind a long counter, school staff members sit at desks with their backs to the waiting area. The principal, vice principal, and counselors' office doors, visible from the waiting area, are shut. At Lake Erie, office staff members frequently appear indifferent to visitors. At their worst, they seem passive-aggressive and disrespectful. A conversation between parents waiting in the main office conveys the effects of this atmosphere on parents:

A parent seated in a plastic chair in the waiting area observes angrily, and loudly enough for everyone in the office to hear, that school staff "always tell you 'come up here,' but don't nobody ever [EXPLETIVE] talk to you when you come." Another parent seated nearby adds indignantly, "It's always been like this— you come up here, and they [EXPLETIVE ignore you, like you ain't [EXPLETIVE]."

In more typical schools like Huron, where student and teacher perceptions of safety are higher, interactions with parents have a very different tone. At Huron, the task of creating a context that encourages mutually respectful and trusting interactions between school staff and parents is undeniably different than at schools like Lake Erie. The response of school staff to that challenge is very different as well. Immediately inside the main office at Huron, a young woman sits at a low receptionist's desk. The office is tidy and well lit; framed posters of natural landscapes are hung on the walls; a water cooler bubbles quietly in a corner. The office staff members respond promptly and respectfully—interactions between parents and school staff appear cordial and professional. Administrators' offices are located immediately across from the waiting area: doors are wide open throughout the office; desks are arranged in the office so that they face the waiting area. Office staff and administrators greet parents with handshakes and smiles. An older man with a distraught, tearful teenage girl in tow is greeted in fluent Spanish by a young woman in dress slacks and a fitted blazer. They speak softly in the waiting area before the woman invites the parent and student into an office, gesturing politely for them to sit.

The contrast between how the main offices at Lake

Erie and Huron are organized and run are clear, as are the differences in how school staff in the two schools approach interactions with parents and visitors. At Lake Erie, where students, parents, and staff frequently appear overwhelmed by the chaos of the school environment, a kind of siege mentality seems to contribute to a closed-off main office, where parents feel unwelcome. Staff at Lake Erie attempt to hold off potential conflict by making it difficult for parents to access teachers and administrators. Yet, this makes the likelihood of conflict worse. Imagine the quality of interactions when a parent finally gets to see a teacher or administrator; the conversation is unlikely to be constructive when either the parent or staff member feels disrespected and defensive. At Huron, despite the real and persistent challenges school staff face in dealing with gang activity, occasional disrespect between students and teachers, and relatively frequent altercations and fights, the main office remains open and respectfully and professionally engaged with students and families.

Case Study

Respectful Interactions with Students Keep Conflicts Manageable

The quality of interactions between school staff and students also differs in high schools like Lake Erie and Huron. In schools like Lake Erie, staff members are often overwhelmed by the magnitude of disorder and disrespect in the school. As they struggle to manage classrooms and hallways, staff members' responses to misbehavior and disrespect become disrespectful themselves.

In the worst cases, sarcastic remarks and thinly veiled insults pass in both directions between students and teachers at Lake Erie. Both adults and children are sensitive to the threat of losing face in front of one another. Adults do not want to lose the respect of other students by allowing a student to treat them disrespectfully, and so they respond in kind to students. Teachers' use of sarcasm, insults, and humiliation rarely calms disruptive or angry students; instead, it escalates conflicts and reinforces negative patterns in student-teacher interactions. This pattern can be seen in field notes from a Lake Erie algebra class, where student disruption prevented the class from going through more than two problems during the period. The teacher's efforts to get students to work by continually telling them they were failing only increased the disrespectful behavior and further disrupted class:

The teacher tries to get another girl to turn around, first by calling her name and then by putting a hand on her shoulder. "Do you want to PASS THIS CLASS?" the teacher shouts, his hand resting on her shoulder. The girl rips her shoulder out from under his hand violently—she leans forward, away from the teacher, and shouts loudly,—"WHY THAT [expletive] ALWAYS TRYIN' TO PUT HIS HANDS ON SOMEBODY?!" The class doesn't react. The teacher stands behind the girl, glaring; her back remains turned, and she goes right on talking to the girls around her without glancing up at the teacher.

The teacher turns to a boy, who is sitting on a desk instead of in his chair, and loudly barks, "DID YOU GET YOUR TEST SCORE (name)? The teacher says pointedly, "You got a 17," and adds, "You have time to talk?" [This does not seem like a friendly request; the teacher's tone is aggressive]. "Gimme my [expletive] test," the boy says angrily. The teacher glares at him, clearly annoyed. "I wish you would," the boy says, standing up suddenly, puffing out his chest and squaring his feet, as though ready to fight. The teacher turns his back on the boy, who continues standing stock-still, staring.

In contrast, school staff at Huron typically respond to student misbehavior in more respectful and thoughtful ways. The opportunity to adopt more strategic responses to student misbehavior at schools like Huron makes it easier for adults to address both serious disruptions and occasional fighting in reflective, respectful ways that quietly diminish conflicts and ratchet down the tension surrounding combustible situations. An instance—where an observer witnesses school staff members responding to a racially charged fight that spills out of the lunchroom one afternoon—illustrates this point:

A number of male students are shouting loudly in the stairwell. Two students among them—one Latino, one African American—are arguing angrily. The first student, his hair disheveled and his shirt un-tucked, shouts heatedly in a mixture of Spanish and English. "Touch me again, [racial slur]," he shouts, "I'll [expletive] you up right here!" The second student, his uniform shirt torn at the collar, shouts back: "[Expletive] you, [racial slur]!" As they shout in the hallway, two security guards in dress slacks and polo shirts arrive and quietly interpose themselves between the boys without touching either of them. They slowly but steadily widen the distance between the students by gently walking each of them back away from the other, while speaking firmly but evenly to the students. Both boys finally turn away, walking in opposite directions, flanked by the security guards.

Case Study

Connections to Adults Offset Safety Concerns for Students

Even within a school as unsafe as Lake Erie, the quality of relationships that students have with their teachers makes a difference for their perceptions of safety and their ability to continue attending class and engaging in learning.

While some students have few teachers they can trust, others are fortunate to have established a good relationship with at least one teacher. For example, the qualitatively different relationships that two Lake Erie students had with their teachers influenced their perceptions of safety in very different ways (excerpts taken from Patton and Johnson, 2010).

Derrick

Derrick, a soft-spoken African American student at Lake Erie, describes an incident he was involved in during the fall of his freshman year. An older student from the same high school assaulted Derrick outside school, beating him and knocking him to the ground, and then subsequently continued to threaten him after school. Wanting to avoid more conflict, Derrick spent the next four weeks leaving his house each morning in his school uniform, only to slip back into his house through the back gate once his mother left for work; all told, he missed almost five full weeks of school during the fall semester.

Derrick's truancy went unnoticed for more than two weeks before a staff member at the school began trying to reach his mother. When he returned to classes, his English teacher had resigned and been replaced with a woman he had never met, who didn't know him; he felt his algebra teacher was unhappy to see him back. Derrick's algebra teacher complained that a lot of the students at Lake Erie, like Derrick, *"don't see education as a priority . . . They don't think it's important for them to be here every day."*

None of Derrick's teachers were informed about the reason for his prolonged absence from his classes, and none of them inquired. Instead, for many of his teachers, Derrick's unexplained absences reinforced their own negative stereotypes about Derrick and students like him: *"Pretty much,"* Derrick's algebra teacher said one afternoon, *"you can give [those kids] work, but they ain't gonna do it."* Derrick felt that his algebra teacher did not like him and went out of his way to pick on him. *"I be payin' attention sometime,"* he explained to an interviewer, *"but [my algebra teacher] just turn[s] on me."*

After feeling like he was being repeatedly singled out in class, Derrick began withdrawing his effort in algebra, and his grades plummeted. *"[My algebra teacher] just get me so mad,"* Derrick explained, *"[that] I say forget it—I'm not doin' this [work] no more."* The weak bond between Derrick and his algebra teacher crumbled quickly; in the absence of any information about who Derrick really was—a shy, vulnerable, and frightened young man—his algebra teacher fashioned a narrative about him in which he was cast as disinterested, unmotivated, and disruptive.

Derrick floundered in a school environment that lacked adult support. He was suspended twice during the spring semester for arguing with his algebra teacher and missed over 35 full days of school that term. He failed every core class both semesters, with the exception of one class in which he earned a D.

Chalise

Chalise, an African American ninth-grader at Lake Erie, had a very different experience, marked by much stronger and more supportive relationships with her teachers. Early in the fall of her freshman year, two of Chalise's close friends from elementary school were shot and killed in gang-related violence. In a very short time, Chalise's attitude towards school seemed to change dramatically—instead of an outgoing, cheerful girl, she became morose and fearful. In her classes, Chalise explained, she often had trouble focusing:

> "[Chris'] desk was right next to mine," she told an interviewer. "I would be ready to do my work, and then all of a sudden, I would think about Chris, [and] then I just started crying." Chalise continued to struggle, despite expressing strong motivation and talking regularly about joining her sister at college—she was distracted and had trouble completing work on time.

However, instead of pulling away from her, Chalise's teachers—and particularly her algebra teacher—knit more closely together around her as she struggled. Her algebra teacher offered to come in early before school to help her complete missed assignments, encouraged her to join a club he sponsored after school, and kept in close contact with her family throughout the year. Chalise slowly rebounded—eventually, her grades improved dramatically, until they exceeded her previous performance in school. She was selected for a national honor society, and one of her teachers observed that she had become one of the few students in her high school class for whom college was obviously attainable. Her algebra teacher said of Chalise, *"She's very independent . . . she's a great kid."*

Even in a chaotic and seemingly disorderly school like Lake Erie, students' experiences and perceptions of their safety are profoundly affected by their connections to adults. While students in schools like Lake Erie struggle, both personally and academically, to make sense of and cope with firsthand experiences of violence and its effects on their families and friends, the connections they are able, or unable, to make with adults in the school community shape their perceptions of safety and their engagement in school.

Disadvantaged Schools with High-Quality Relationships Feel as Safe as Advantaged Schools with Weak Relationships

As this chapter has shown, the quality of relationships within the school community – among students, teachers, and families—matters greatly for students' and teachers' feelings of safety. As shown in Figures 15–17, regardless of the overall advantage level of the school (defined by school achievement and poverty and by crime and human resources in students' neighborhoods), safety is better where there are higher-quality relationships among students, teachers, and families. This holds true across all three indicators of school safety.

Indeed, high-quality relationships within schools help make up for serving students with greater disadvantages. Schools that serve the least advantaged students, yet have very strong relationships among students, teachers, and parents, are *safer* than schools that serve the most advantaged students yet have weak relationships, based on student reports of safety and teacher perceptions of crime and disorder. The one exception is in the quality of peer interactions, where the quality of relationships does not completely make up for the differences between schools serving the most advantaged and disadvantaged students.

To put these differences into perspective, recall Pacific, Huron, and Lake Erie high schools. A school serving students with few advantages—with low incoming achievement levels and many students coming from neighborhoods with high rates of poverty and crime—would be very unlikely to resemble Pacific, a very safe school, regardless of the quality of relationships within the school. However, if that school had strong relationships among parents, teachers, and students, it would be more likely to resemble Huron—where there are some problems with fights and disrespect, but most students feel safe within the school—than Lake Erie—where there are frequent fights, substantial disrespect among students and staff, and half of students feel unsafe in the hallways and bathrooms.

Likewise, a school that served relatively advantaged students might have the opportunity to provide a very safe environment for students, such as the climate in

FIGURE 15

Students report feeling safer in schools with strong relationships

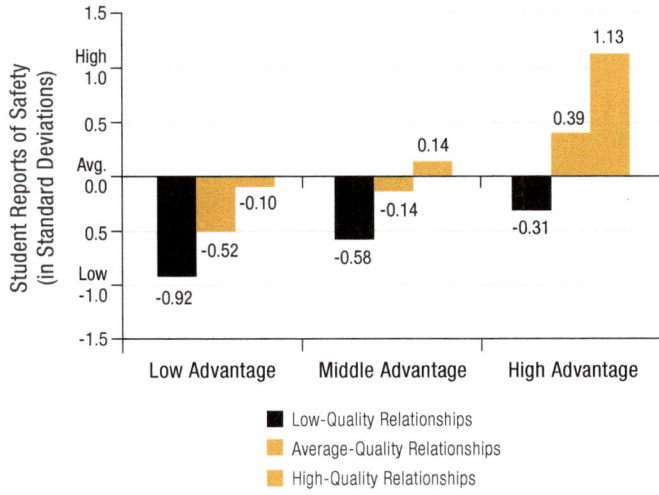

Note: The values reported are the mean level of school safety as reported by students, in standard deviation units. A school's level of *Advantage* depends on the level of crime, poverty, and human and social resources in their students' home neighborhoods and the school academic achievement. A school's quality of *Relationships* depends on the quality of its *School-Family Interactions*, as perceived by teachers, and *Student-Teacher Relationships*, as perceived by students. Among *Low Advantage* schools, there are 95 schools with *Low-Quality Relationships*, 67 schools with *Average-Quality Relationships* and 17 schools with *High-Quality Relationships*. Among *Middle Advantage* schools, there are 59 schools with *Low-Quality Relationships*, 58 schools with *Average-Quality Relationships* and 36 schools with *High-Quality Relationships*. Among *High Advantage* schools, there are 15 schools with *Low-Quality Relationships*, 51 schools with *Average-Quality Relationships* and 126 schools with *High-Quality Relationships*.

FIGURE 16

Teachers report less crime and disorder in schools with strong relationships

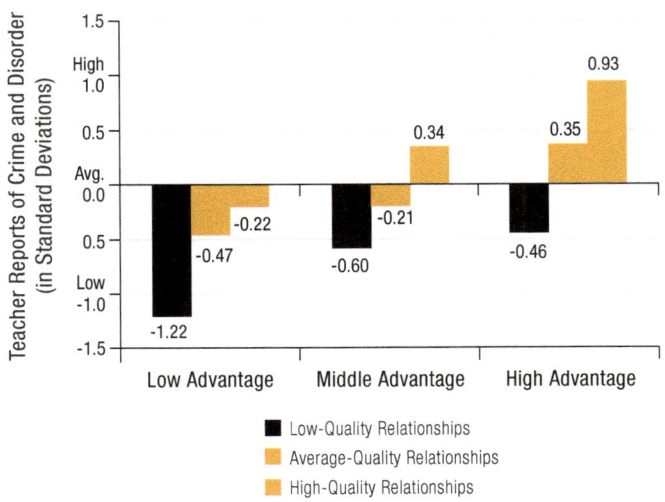

Note: The values reported are the mean level of crime and disorder as reported by teachers, in standard deviation units. A school's level of *Advantage* depends on the level of crime, poverty, and human and social resources in their students' home neighborhoods and the school academic achievement. A school's quality of *Relationships* depends on the quality of its *School-Family Interactions*, as perceived by teachers, and *Student-Teacher Relationships*, as perceived by students. Among *Low Advantage* schools, there are 59 schools with *Low-Quality Relationships*, 48 schools with *Average-Quality Relationships* and 13 schools with *High-Quality Relationships*. Among *Middle Advantage* schools, there are 45 schools with *Low-Quality Relationships*, 44 schools with *Average-Quality Relationships* and 31 schools with *High-Quality Relationships*. Among *High Advantage* schools, there are 12 schools with *Low-Quality Relationships*, 42 schools with *Average-Quality Relationships* and 93 schools with *High-Quality Relationships*.

FIGURE 17

Students report more positive peer interactions in schools with high-quality relationships

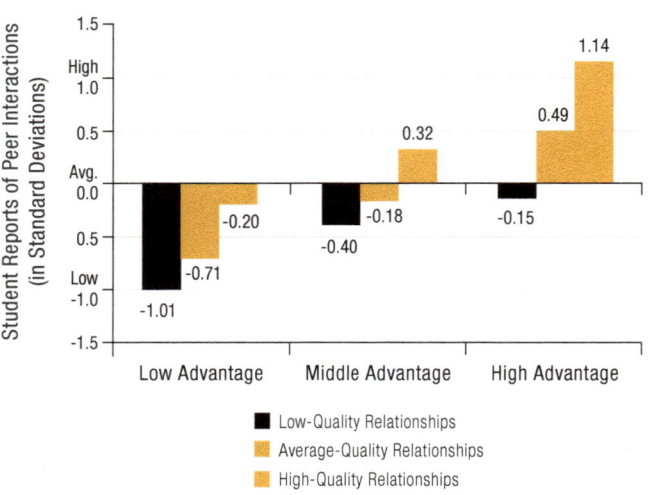

- Low-Quality Relationships
- Average-Quality Relationships
- High-Quality Relationships

Note: The values reported are the mean level of peer interactions, as reported by students, in standard deviation units. A school's level of *Advantage* depends on the level of crime, poverty, and human and social resources in their students' home neighborhoods and the school academic achievement. A school's quality of *Relationships* depends on the quality of its *School-Family Interactions*, as perceived by teachers, and *Student-Teacher Relationships*, as perceived by students. Among *Low Advantage* schools, there are 95 schools with *Low-Quality Relationships*, 67 schools with *Average-Quality Relationships* and 17 schools with *High-Quality Relationships*. Among *Middle Advantage* schools, there are 59 schools with *Low-Quality Relationships*, 58 schools with *Average-Quality Relationships* and 36 schools with *High-Quality Relationships*. Among *High Advantage* schools, there are 15 schools with *Low-Quality Relationships*, 51 schools with *Average-Quality Relationships* and 126 schools with *High-Quality Relationships*.

Pacific, where the vast majority of students feel safe in all areas within the school and there are few problems with physical conflicts or disrespect of teachers. However, to do so, it would need to develop and maintain strong relationships among parents, teachers, and students; otherwise, it would be more likely to resemble Huron, with substantial, but not overwhelming, threats to safety among students and teachers.

The backgrounds and skills students bring with them to school set the context in which school staff work, so that school staff who serve highly disadvantaged students must be more strategic than those at schools serving more advantaged students. At the same time, their likelihood of reacting to conflict and disorder in a way that aggravates problems is higher, as they must respond to a larger quantity of issues on an ongoing basis. Simply put, their job is much harder and requires more skill. How they respond to issues of conflict matters immensely for the ability of teachers and students to feel safe in their school and productively engage in the process of teaching and learning.

Chapter 4

Interpretive Summary

School safety is a critical policy issue in Chicago and across the country. In Chicago, the district has focused on creating and implementing culture of calm to address the violence and disorder that exist in many schools. Up to this point, however, the extent to which students and teachers report feeling unsafe and the factors contributing to such feelings have been largely unknown. This report characterizes the extent of the problem across Chicago schools, the socioeconomic and institutional factors influencing school safety, and the social-organizational factors within schools that mediate the adverse influences of neighborhood and community disadvantage on school safety. The goals of the report are to show the scope of the problem of school safety in Chicago and provide evidence on which to base decisions about policy and practice.

> Punitive measures are less likely to be effective than measures that build and foster respect and trust.

Chapter 1 presents evidence on the state of safety across Chicago elementary and high schools. The findings suggest that safety is an urgent issue at both the elementary and high school levels for both students and teachers in Chicago schools. Nearly half of teachers in grades K–8 reported significant problems related to disorder in the classrooms and hallways, physical conflicts among students, and student disrespect of teachers. More than half of high school teachers reported problems associated with robbery or theft in the school, and over 60 percent reported problems with gang activity, disorder in the classrooms and hallways, physical conflicts among students, and student disrespect of teachers. In addition, more than one-quarter of high school teachers reported student threats of violence toward teachers in their school. While some schools in Chicago struggle with serious safety issues, others are safe environments for students and teachers. By understanding why there are differences in safety across schools, we can see possible mechanisms through which safety concerns might be best addressed.

One dimension that affects students' feelings of safety, and their reports of positive interactions among peers, is the extent to which adults are present. Schools need to pay particular attention to the areas where there is typically little or no adult supervision, particularly in the area just outside of the school building. The vast majority of CPS students feel safe in their classrooms; however, many of the same students feel unsafe in areas immediately outside of the school building. The area of the schoolyard is of more concern to students than are the routes coming and going to school. Compared with students' paths coming and going to school, the area just outside the school is one where it is easier to coordinate supervision. Improvements in safety in the area around the school would likely go a long way toward improving students' feelings of safety at school.

Adults—not just school staff, but adults in students' home communities and in their families—play very important roles in determining the climate of safety in schools. Broadly speaking, students' families, peer groups, neighborhood and community characteristics, and school setting all work together to shape students' academic and behavioral development, and the overall climate in schools. From Chapter 2, we see that the characteristics that students bring with them from their home neighborhoods are strongly related to the climate of safety within schools, and these characteristics are much more important than structural features of the school itself, such as its location, size, or grade level. As might be expected, crime and poverty in students' residential neighborhoods are strongly associated with school safety. Neighborhoods with high crime and poverty tend to have fewer human and social resources available to students, and these social resources lead students to feel safe as they travel between home and school and as they manage conflicts with peers.

The findings from Chapter 2 also indicate that a school's level of academic achievement is the contextual factor that most strongly defines safety for both students and teachers. This is not simply because students learn less in schools with poor learning climates.

Indeed, for high schools we show the relationship between school safety and students' academic achievement prior to high school; for elementary schools, we use prior achievement (e.g., fifth grade) for the sixth- through eighth-grade students responding to the CCSR survey. The influence of poverty and crime on school safety operates to a great extent through the achievement level of students in the school—students from more advantaged neighborhoods are more likely to attend higher-achieving schools, while students from disadvantaged neighborhoods are likely to attend low-achieving schools.

The strong relationship between school achievement level and school safety may seem surprising—particularly because it is more important than crime or poverty. But it makes sense for a number of reasons. One reason is the degree to which students are attached to school: high-achieving students tend to be engaged in learning and feel successful academically, while students with low levels of achievement are less likely to be engaged academically and more likely to feel frustrated by their performance.[49] This, in turn, makes lower-achieving students more likely to act out and less likely to respond to academic punishments. Indeed, the salience of academic consequences for misbehavior may be minimal for students who are already poorly engaged in learning—if students do not care about school, suspension is not a powerful deterrent.[50] Second, to the extent that academic achievement reflects general intelligence, students who have greater cognitive skills also have the ability to bring those to bear on solving complex social interactions and situations.[51] When students lack these skills, they are more likely to use less adaptive coping strategies, such as resorting to physical and verbal aggression. Finally, students with lower academic achievement often have experienced higher levels of disruption outside of school—family disruption, violence, and stress. These factors influence both student achievement and the likelihood of acting out and engaging in disruptive behaviors.[52] Students living in high-poverty and high-crime neighborhoods are particularly vulnerable and likely to experience disruption, and those students are likely to exhibit both low academic achievement and more behavioral problems. This is consistent with a research finding that the biggest benefit to students from selecting a higher-achieving school rather than a neighborhood school was in the decreased likelihood of trouble with police.[53]

The schools that most need resources and interventions to address issues of school climate are not necessarily those that are located in the poorest neighborhoods, but those serving students with the lowest levels of achievement. This suggests that district leaders should target schools with very low academic capital. Policies that cluster students into schools based on their achievement need to recognize these safety concerns for schools serving low-achieving students. This also suggests a vicious cycle—schools need to search for ways to make students with low incoming achievement more invested and successful in school in order to promote safer schooling environments. Yet, it is more difficult for students to focus on learning, and for teachers to teach effectively, when the school environment is unsafe and disorderly.

The good news from Chapter 2 is that demographics are not destiny. Schools serving very similar students can have very different levels of safety. Indeed, the findings from Chapter 3 suggest that inside the school building, the mutually supportive relationships that students and their parents have with teachers are the most critical elements defining school safety for both students and teachers. Much of what accounts for the large differences in school safety among schools in Chicago are the ways in which parents, teachers, and students work together collaboratively. Schools are safer when teachers view parents as supportive partners in children's education. When students feel that their teachers care about their learning and overall well-being and listen to them, students and teachers alike report safer school environments.

In contrast, punitive measures are less likely to be effective than measures that build and foster respect and trust. High rates of suspension do not show any benefit for either students' or teachers' feelings of safety at school, and they may even have adverse effects on school climate by aggravating distrust between students and adults. Thus, the approach of culture of calm seems to be a step in the right direction, as it encourages schools to develop mechanisms to build relationships with students and their families, rather than relying predominantly on punitive mechanisms. This approach is also consistent with the framework of Positive Behavioral Intervention and Supports (PBIS), which promotes effective, data-driven practices around school disciplinary practices. PBIS is supported by the U.S. Department of Education and by recent research.[54] In contrast to reactive discipline, PBIS is based on designing school and classroom systems that establish a social climate that supports teaching and learning and prevents problematic behavior, with secondary and tertiary supports for students with problem behaviors.[55] Such an approach requires a substantial change in practice, though, including time for planning and coordination with support and professional development.

School-based relationships are critical in overcoming school-level disadvantage for creating safe schooling environments. Among the most disadvantaged schools with the highest-quality relationships, school climates are at least as safe as the most advantaged schools with the weakest school-based relationships. The gap in safety between schools with middle and high levels of advantage (in terms of poverty, crime, or achievement) is completely overcome by the quality of school-based relationships. CPS schools that serve typical students from typical neighborhoods are as safe as schools serving the most advantaged students in the system if their schools have cultivated strong partnerships with parents, and between teachers and students.

Adults—teachers and parents—matter a great deal to the safety of schools. They not only matter for people's physical safety at school, but also for the quality of students' relationships with each other. Students are more respectful and helpful to each other the more that there are adults present with whom they have trusting relationships. Students in schools with the most problematic student interactions—low-achieving schools, and schools that are predominantly African American—particularly need guidance and support from adults to help navigate peer-to-peer interactions and issues that may result in conflict.

This means that staffing levels need to be sufficient in schools with large safety concerns to keep teachers and other staff members from feeling overwhelmed. Moreover, adults need training to break the escalating cycles of disrespect that contribute to unsafe environments for students, teachers, and parents. Faculty and staff in very low-achieving schools require skills in managing conflict, and time and resources for strategically managing disruption and violence, so that students, their parents, and teachers can productively work together. It suggests that district and school leaders need to be strategic about building internal school structures that encourage productive dialogue among adults and students. It also suggests the need for resources and training for teachers and other school personnel to develop competencies in coping with tense and potentially disruptive and violent interactions that may occur within schools.

In addition to the primacy of school-based relationships among students, teachers, and parents, the form and quality of leadership in the school plays a role in how teachers perceive crime and disorder. Teachers view their schools as safer when they are more involved in school-based decision making, and when they observe that school programs are coordinated with the school's goals for instruction and student learning. These factors affect safety largely through the quality of relationships that teachers develop with parents and students as they work with colleagues on school improvement. Thus, teacher professionalism can also play an important role in producing more positive and constructive learning environments for their students.

While this report paints a picture of concern about school safety in many Chicago schools, it does suggest that how schools operate can make a difference. The efforts of principals, teachers, families, and policymakers to create a safer schooling setting is difficult in some places, such as schools with lower average student achievement and those serving more disadvantaged populations of students. However, student demographics and the extent of poverty and crime they experience outside school do not solely determine the extent of safety in their schools. What comes out most clearly is the importance of social relationships and cooperative work for creating a safe, orderly environment—through social resources in the community, a shared commitment among teachers, the building of trusting relationships with students, and partnerships with parents. Schools do not choose which students they serve, but the ways in which they set up interactions with parents, respond to conflicts among students, and build collaboration among staff do much to determine the climate in which students and teachers do their work.

References

Allensworth, Elaine, Stephen Ponisciak, and Christopher Mazzeo (2009)
The Schools Teachers Leave: Teacher Mobility in Chicago Public Schools. Consortium on Chicago School Research.

American Psychological Association Zero Tolerance Task Force (2008)
Are Zero Tolerance Policies Effective in Schools? An Evidentiary Review and Recommendations. *American Psychologist*, 63(9), 852–62.

Astor, Ron Avi, Nancy Guerra, and Richard Van Acker (2010)
How Can We Improve School Safety Research? *Educational Researcher*, 39(1), 69–78.

Astor, Ron Avi, Rami Benbenishty, and Jose Nuñez Estrada (2009)
School Violence and Theoretically Atypical Schools: The Principal's Centrality in Orchestrating Safe Schools. *American Educational Research Journal*, 46(2), 423–61.

Bogenschneider, Karen (1996)
An Ecological Risk/Protective Theory for Building Prevention Programs, Policies, and Community Capacity to Support Youth. *Family Relations*, 45(2), 127–38.

Borum, Randy, Dewey G. Cornell, William Modzeleski, and Shane R. Jimerson (2010)
What Can Be Done About School Shootings? A Review of the Evidence. *Educational Researcher*, 39(1), 27–37.

Bowen, Natasha K., and Gary L. Bowen (1999)
Effects of Crime and Violence in Neighborhoods and Schools on the School Behavior and Performance of Adolescents. *Journal of Adolescent Research*, 14(3), 319–42.

Bowen, Natasha K., Gary L. Bowen, and William B. Ware (2002)
Neighborhood Social Disorganization, Families, and the Educational Behavior of Adolescents. *Journal of Adolescent Research*, 17(5), 468–90.

Bronfenbrenner, Urie (1979)
The Ecology of Human Development. Cambridge, MA: Harvard University Press.

Brooks-Gunn, Jeanne, Greg J. Duncan, Pamela K. Klebanov, and Naomi Sealand (1993)
Do Neighborhoods Influence Child and Adolescent Development? *The American Journal of Sociology*, 99(2), 353–95.

Bryk, Anthony S., and Barbara L. Schneider (2002)
Trust in Schools: *A Core Resource for Improvement.* New York: Russell Sage Foundation.

Bryk, Anthony S., Penny Bender Sebring, Elaine Allensworth, Stuart Luppescu, and John Q. Easton (2010)
Organizing Schools for Improvement: Lessons from Chicago. Chicago: The University of Chicago Press.

Crosnoe, Robert, Monica K. Johnson, and Glen H. Elder Jr. (2004)
Intergenerational Bonding in School: The Behavioral and Contextual Correlates of Student-Teacher Relationships. *Sociology of Education*, 77(1), 60–81.

Cullen, Julie B., Brian A. Jacob, and Steven D. Levitt (2003)
The Effect of School Choice on Student Outcomes: Evidence from Randomized Lotteries. Cambridge, MA: National Bureau of Economic Research working paper series no. 10113.

Dinkes, Rachel, Jana Kemp, and Katrina Baum (2009)
Indicators of School Crime and Safety: 2008 (NCES 2009–022/NCJ 226343). National Center for Education Statistics, Institute of Education Sciences, U.S. Department of Education, and Bureau of Justice Statistics, Office of Justice Programs, U.S. Department of Justice. Washington, DC.

Epstein, Joyce L., and Mavis G. Sanders (2000)
Connecting Home, School, and Community: New Directions for Social Research, In Maureen T. Hallinan (Ed.), *Handbook of the Sociology of Education*, 285-306, New York: Kluwer Academic/Plenum Publishers.

Felson, Richard B., Allen E. Liska, Scott J. South, and Thomas L. McNulty (1994)
The Subculture of Violence and Delinquency: Individual vs. School Context Effects. *Social Forces*, 73(1), 155–73.

Forehand, R., K. S. Miller, and R. Dutra (1997)
Role of Parenting in Adolescent Deviant Behavior: Replication across and within Two Ethnic Groups. *Journal of Consulting and Clinical Psychology*, 65, 1036–41.

Graber, J. A., T. Nichols, and S. D. Lynne (2006)
A Longitudinal Examination of Family, Friend, and Media Influences on Competent Versus Problem Behaviors among Urban Minority Youth. *Applied Developmental Science*, 10, 75–85.

Harris Interactive and GLSEN (2005)
From Teasing to Torment: School Climate in America, A Survey of Students and Teachers. New York: GLSEN.

Hatch, J. Amos (2002)
Doing Qualitative Research in Education Settings. Albany, NY: State University of New York Press.

Horner, Robert H., George Sugai, Keith Smolkowski, Lucille Eber, Jean Nakasato, Anne W. Todd, and Jody Esperanza (2009)
A Randomized, Wait-List Controlled Effectiveness Trial Assessing School-Wide Positive Behavior Support in Elementary Schools, *Journal of Positive Behavior Interventions*, 11(3), 133–44.

Kazdin, A. E. (2000)
Behavior Modification in Applied Settings. (6th ed.) Pacific Grove, CA: Brooks/Cole.

LeCompte, Margaret D., and Judity Preissle (1993)
Ethnography and Qualitative Design in Educational Research. 2nd ed. New York, NY: Academic Press.

Loeber, Rolf, and Dale Hay (1997)
Key Issues in the Development of Aggression and Violence from Childhood to Early Adulthood. *Annual Review of Psychology*, 48, 371–410.

Macmillan, Ross, and John Hagan (2004)
Violence in the Transition to Adulthood: Adolescent Victimization, Education, and Socioeconomic Attainment in Later Life. *Journal of Research on Adolescence*, 14(2), 127–58.

Meyers, S. A., and C. Miller (2004)
Direct, Mediated, Moderated, and Cumulative Relations between neighborhood Characteristics and Adolescent Outcomes. *Adolescence*, 39, 121–44.

Miles, Matthew B., and A. Michael Huberman (1994)
Qualitative Data Analysis. Thousand Oaks, CA: Sage Publications.

Neiman, Samantha, and Jill F. DeVoe (2009)
Crime, Violence, Discipline, and Safety in U.S. Public Schools: Findings From the School Survey on Crime and Safety: 2007–08 (NCES 2009-326). National Center for Education Statistics, Institute of Education Sciences, U.S. Department of Education. Washington, DC.

Newmann, Fred M., Gary G. Wehlage, and Susie D. Lamborn (2002)
The Significance and Sources of Student Engagement. In Fred M. Newmann (Ed.). *Student Engagement and Achievement in American Secondary Schools* (11–39). New York: Teachers College, Columbia University.

Osher, David, George G. Bear, Jeffrey R. Sprague, and Walter Doyle (2010)
How Can We Improve School Discipline? *Educational Researcher*, 39(1), 48–58.

Payne, Allison A., Denise C. Gottfredson, and Gary D. Gottfredson (2003)
Schools as Communities: The Relationships Among Communal School Organization, Student Bonding, and School Disorder. *Criminology*, 41(3), 749–77.

Rand, Michael R. (December, 2008)
National Crime Victimization Survey: Criminal Victimization, 2007. Bureau of Justice Statistics, U.S. Department of Justice. Washington, DC.

Sampson, Robert J., Stephen W. Raudenbush, and Felton Earls (1997)
Neighborhoods and Violent Crime: A Multilevel Study of Collective Efficacy. *Science*, 77(5328), 918–24.

Schreck, Christopher J., and J. Mitchell Miller (2003)
Sources of Fear of Crime at School: What Is the Relative Contribution of Disorder, Individual Characteristics, and School Security? *Journal of School Violence*, 2(4), 57–79.

Sergiovanni, Thomas J. (2004)
The Lifeworld of Leadership: Creating Culture, Community, and Personal Meaning in Our Schools. San Francisco: Josey-Bass.

Singh, Kusu, Monique Granville, and Sandra Dika (2002)
Mathematics and science achievement: Effects of motivation, interest and academic engagement. *The Journal of Educational Research*, 95(6), 323–32.

Smith, Deborah L., and Brian J. Smith (2006)
Perceptions of Violence: The Views of Teachers Who Left Urban Schools. *The High School Journal*, 89(3), 34–42.

Smokowski, Paul R., and Kelly Holland Kopasz (2005)
Bullying in School: An Overview of Types, Effects, Family Characteristics, and Intervention Strategies. *Children & Schools*, 27(2), 101–9.

Swearer, Susan M., Dorothy L. Espelage, Tracy Vaillancourt, and Shelley Hymel (2010)
What Can be Done About School Bullying? Linking Research to Educational Practice. *Educational Researcher*, 39(1), 38–47.

Welsh, Wayne N. (2000)
The Effects of School Climate on School Disorder. *The ANNALS of the American Academy of Political and Social Science*, 567(1), 88–107.

Welsh, Wayne N., Jack R. Greene, and Patricia H. Jenkins (1999)
School Disorder: The Influence of Individual, Institutional, and Community Factors. *Criminology*, 37(1), 73–115.

Welsh, Wayne N., Robert Stokes, and Jack R. Greene (2000)
A Macro-Level Model of School Disorder. *Journal of Research in Crime and Delinquency*, 37(3), 243–83.

Appendix A:
Student and Teacher Survey Responses

Statistics on safety were adjusted for the response rates of students and teachers at each school. Responses were weighted by the inverse of their school's response rate on the 2009 survey (e.g., $\text{Weight}_i = 1/\text{ResponseRate}_j$, where i indexes either student or teacher, and j indexes school). The adjusted school response rates were used when showing the distribution of item responses on the survey measures for students in grades six to 12 and teachers in grades K–12, in Figures 1–3. Only schools with non-zero response rates on the 2009 CCSR survey were included, and analyses were performed to ensure that the statistics were not biased by non-response among schools. Because of high rates of participation at the school level, this was not a source of bias, as described further under survey representativeness.

The table below summarizes the sample sizes and response rates for each of the three survey measures by school level. For *Student Reports of Safety* and *Student Reports of Peer Interactions*, elementary school student respondents include students in grades six to eight in the 2008–09 school year and high school respondents include students in grades nine to 12 in the 2008–09 school year. For *Teacher Reports of Crime and Disorder*, elementary school teacher respondents include all elementary school teachers in grades K–8 and high school teacher respondents include all high school teachers in grades nine to 12, both during the 2008–09 school year.

Sample sizes for *Student Reports of Safety* and *Student Reports of Peer Interactions* are the average number of students who responded to the items comprising each survey measure on the 2009 survey; for *Teacher Reports of Crime and Disorder*, sample size is the average number of teachers who responded to the items comprising this survey measure on the 2009 survey. The response rate is the share of all students (for *Student Reports of Safety* and *Student Reports of Peer Interactions*) and teachers (for *Teacher Reports of Crime and Disorder*) in CPS, by school level, who responded to the survey. At the school level, 88.5 percent (462 of 522) of elementary schools and 84.6 percent (115 of 136) of high schools had a non-zero response rate on the student survey, while 86.2 percent (450 of 522) of elementary schools and 85.3 percent (116 of 136) of high schools had a non-zero response rate on the teacher survey.

TABLE 8

District-wide response rates

School Level	Student Reports of Safety		Student Reports of Peer Interactions		Teacher Reports of Crime and Disorder	
	Sample Size	Response Rate	Sample Size	Response Rate	Sample Size	Response Rate
Elementary	65,007	59.2%	64,692	59.2%	8,774	52.0%
High School	52,478	49.4%	51,854	49.4%	3,965	53.8%

Note: The sample size is the average number of teachers or students responding to each survey measure. For example, four items comprise *Student Reports of Safety*, and in some cases all student respondents did not respond to each item. As such, the sample size reflects the average number responding to each item within a survey measure. The response rate is the percentage of students or teachers who responded to at least one item for a given survey measure.

Survey Representativeness

We examined the extent to which the observed student and teacher responses on the measures of school safety represent CPS system-wide, since all students and teachers did not participate in the 2009 CCSR survey. We tested for systematic non-response for both the student and teacher surveys by modeling school-level student and teacher response rates as a function of safety on the other survey. In other words, we modeled the teacher response rate as a function of *student* reports of safety, and the student response rate as a function of *teacher* reports of crime and disorder. This is possible because non-response at the school level was different for the student survey than for the teacher survey. The logic underlying this analysis was to assess whether, and to what extent, student response rates vary with the level of safety in the school, as captured by how teachers perceive safety, and vice-versa. If student reports of safety predict teacher response rates, we would have reason to believe that students in schools with different levels of safety are responding to the CCSR survey at different rates, that systematic bias in response rates exists as a function of school safety levels, and that our estimates of safety from the observed surveys may mischaracterize safety across Chicago schools. The reverse would be true for student response rates. We found that whether or not schools participated in the student or teacher survey—that is, if schools had a non-zero response rate on either the student or teacher survey—was unrelated to the level of safety, as reported by the opposite group.

However, while we did not find a systematic bias in whether schools participated, there was a small relationship between safety and response rates across schools. Elementary school teachers and students, and high school students (not teachers), were more likely to respond to the survey when their schools were safer. In particular, response rates among elementary school teachers differ, on average, by approximately 5 percentage points across schools that differ on elementary school student reports of safety by one standard deviation. For elementary school students, response rates differ, on average, by 6 percentage points across schools that differ on teacher reports of crime and disorder by one standard deviation. High school student response rates differ, on average, by 9 percentage points across schools that differ on high school teacher reports of crime and disorder by one standard deviation. These differences are likely due to lower attendance rates in schools that are less safe.

On balance, evidence suggests that students and teachers at safer schools were slightly more likely to respond to the 2009 CCSR survey. Therefore, the district-wide statistics are calculated by weighting student and teacher response by the school response rates to address potential bias from slightly lower response rates at less safe schools.

TABLE 9
Relationships between response rates and safety

Independent Variable	Dependent Variable (school level)	Coefficient	Sample Size	Mean (S.D.) of Dependent Variable
Teacher Reports of Crime and Disorder	Student Response Rate (Elementary)	0.059***	320	0.829 (0.183)
	Student Response Rate (High School)	0.094***	68	0.609 (0.246)
Student Reports of Safety	Teacher Response Rate (Elementary)	0.049***	448	0.545 (0.293)
	Teacher Response Rate (High School)	-0.029	76	0.612 (0.265)

Note: Coefficients from a bivariate regression of the dependent variable (teacher or student response rate at the school level) on the safety measure (for teacher response rates the independent variable is *Student Reports of Safety*; for student response rates the independent variable is *Teacher Reports of Crime and Disorder*). Coefficients are statistically significant at the *10 percent, **5 percent and ***1 percent levels.

Appendix B:
Survey Measures Used in This Report

TABLE 10

Survey measures and questions

CCSR Survey Measure	Survey Questions
Student Perceptions of Safety (s) reliability = .63	How safe do you feel: • Outside around the school • Traveling between home and school • In the hallways and bathrooms of the school • In your classes
Teacher Perceptions of Crime and Disorder (t) reliability = .88	To what extent is each of the following a problem at your school: • Physical conflicts among students • Robbery or theft • Gang activity • Disorder in classrooms • Disorder in hallways • Student disrespect of teachers • Threats of violence toward teachers
Student Perceptions of Peer Interactions (s) reliability = .62	Most students in my school: • Don't really care about each other • Like to put others down • Help each other learn • Don't get along together very well • Just look out for themselves • Treat each other with respect
Teacher Influence (t) reliability = .81	How much influence do teachers have over school policy in each of the areas below? • Determining books and other instructional materials used in classrooms. • Determining the content of in-service programs. • Establishing the curriculum and instructional program. • Hiring new professional personnel. • Planning how discretionary school funds should be used. • Setting standards for student behavior.

TABLE 10

Continued

CCSR Survey Measure	Survey Questions
Principal Instructional Leadership (t) *reliability = .90*	**Please mark the extent to which you disagree or agree with each of the following:** **The principal at this school:** • Makes clear to the staff his or her expectations for meeting instructional goals. • Communicates a clear vision for our school. • Sets high standards for teaching. • Understands how children learn. • Presses teachers to implement what they have learned in professional development. • Carefully tracks student academic progress. • Knows what's going on in my classroom. • Participates in instructional planning with teams of teachers
Program Coherence (t) *reliability = .74*	**Please mark the extent to which you disagree or agree with each of the following:** • Curriculum, instruction, and learning materials are well coordinated across the different grade levels at this school. • Many special programs come and go at this school. • Once we start a new program, we follow-up to make sure that it's working. • We have so many different programs in this school that I can't keep track of them all. • There is consistency in curriculum, instruction, and learning materials among teachers in the same grade level at this school.
Teacher-Principal Trust (t) *reliability = .76*	**Please mark the extent to which you disagree or agree with each of the following:** **The principal at this school:** • Is an effective manager who makes the school run smoothly. • The principal places the needs of children ahead of personal and political interests. • I trust the principal at his or her word. • It's OK in this school to discuss feelings, worries, and frustrations with the principal. • The principal has confidence in the expertise of the teachers. • The principal looks out for the personal welfare of the faculty members. • The principal takes a personal interest in the professional development of teachers. **To what extent do you feel respected by:** • Your principal?

TABLE 10
Continued

CCSR Survey Measure	Survey Questions
Collective Responsibility (t) reliability = .91	**How many teachers in this school:** • Feel responsible for helping students develop self-control? • Feel responsible that all students learn? • Feel responsible to help each other do their best? • Feel responsible when students in this school fail? • Help maintain discipline in the entire school, not just their classroom? • Take responsibility for improving the school?
Orientation to Innovation (t) reliability = .87	**How many teachers in this school:** • Are eager to try new ideas? • Are really trying to improve their teaching? • Are willing to take risks to make this school better? **Please mark the extent to which you disagree or agree with each of the following:** • All teachers are encouraged to "stretch and grow." • In this school, teachers are continually learning and seeking new ideas.
Socialization of New Teachers (t) reliability = .54	**Please mark the extent to which you disagree or agree with each of the following:** • Experienced teachers invite new teachers into their rooms to observe, give feedback, etc. • A conscious effort is made by faculty to make new teachers feel welcome here.
Teacher-Teacher Trust (t) reliability = .63	**Please mark the extent to which you disagree or agree with each of the following:** • It's OK in this school to discuss feelings, worries, and frustrations with other teachers. • Teachers at this school respect those colleagues who are expert at their craft. • Teachers in this school trust each other. • Teachers respect other teachers who take the lead in school improvement efforts. **To what extent do you feel respected by:** • Other teachers?
Human and Social Resources in the Community (s) reliability = .68	**How much do you agree with the following statements about the community in which you live:** • There are adults in this neighborhood that children can look up to. • Adults in this neighborhood know who the local children are. • You can count on adults in this neighborhood to see that children are safe and do not get into trouble. • During the day, it is safe for children to play in the local park or playground. • People in this neighborhood can be trusted. • The equipment and buildings in the neighborhood park or playground are well kept.

TABLE 10

Continued

CCSR Survey Measure	Survey Questions
Teacher-Parent Trust (t) *reliability = .76*	**For the students you teach this year, how many of their parents:** • Support your teaching efforts? **How many teachers in this school:** • Feel good about parents' support for their work? **Please mark the extent to which you disagree or agree with each of the following statements about your school:** • Staff at this school work hard to build trusting relationships with parents. • Teachers and parents think of each other as partners in educating children. **To what extent do you feel respected by:** • The parents of your students? **For the students you teach this year, how many of their parents:** • Do their best to help their children learn
Teacher Personal Support (s) *reliability = .81*	**The teacher for this class:** • Really listens to what I have to say • Is willing to give extra help on schoolwork if I need it • Helps me catch up if I am behind • Believes I can do well in school
Student-Teacher Trust (s) *reliability = .63*	**Please mark the extent to which you disagree or agree with each of the following:** • My teachers always keeps his/her promises • My teachers always try to be fair • I feel safe and comfortable with my teachers at this school • When my teachers tell me not to do something, I know he/she has a good reason • My teachers will always listen to students' ideas • My teachers treat me with respect **My teachers:** • Really care about me • The teacher for this class really cares about me

Appendix C:
Methodological Details on Statistical Models

Adjustments for Measurement and Sampling Error

All of the analyses were conducted at the school level, using mean levels of safety as reported by students or teachers. When using survey responses, there are multiple sources of error in the estimate of school climate. One source comes from the ways in which individual respondents fill out the surveys; for example, a person may not fill out all of the questions about safety, or may misread a question and respond in the opposite way intended. A second source of error comes from less than complete response rates at the school—if not all students or teachers at the school participate in the survey, we may not gain a completely accurate sense of the climate since we do not include all people's perceptions. To adjust for the first source of error, we use Rasch modeling techniques to create individuals' scores on the climate measures that produces a standard error for each individual based on the ways in which they responded to the questions. Responses that are incomplete or irregular (i.e., indicating that they misread a question) receive a larger standard error. We then use the standard error to adjust for the degree to which that person's score is likely to be accurate when constructing the school mean. The school means are constructed through hierarchical models in which the first level is the measurement model that uses the standard error. The second level is students or teachers, and the third level is schools. The school estimate is a precision-weighted Bayesian estimate, which takes into account the second source of error—the number of responses in a school. Schools with smaller response rates are "shrunk" towards the grand mean of the system, since there is less confidence that the school is properly represented.

The school-level Bayesian estimates were used for all analyses in this report. Analysis of the relationships of contextual factors and social-organizational factors with safety used OLS regression models, predicting the Bayesian estimates with school-level contextual variables and similarly-constructed Baysian estimates of school social-organizational factors, measured from surveys.

Statistical Models for Changes in School Safety since 2007

We examined whether Chicago schools became safer, on average, between the 2007 and 2009 administrations of the CCSR survey by exploring the change in the three survey measures (*Student Reports of Safety*, *Student Reports of Peer Interactions*, and *Teacher Reports of Crime and Disorder*) using three-level unconditional hierarchical models. The hierarchical structure of the models allows schools to be compared to themselves, eliminating any bias that may result from different schools participating in each survey year. Level-1 was a measurement model, Level-2 modeled students or teachers, and Level-3 modeled schools. Years were entered as dummy variables in the Level-1 measurement model. The student measures were available in years prior to 2007, and models were run that included these earlier years. However, teacher reports of crime and disorder have only been available since 2007.

Level-1 Model

$Y = P1*(WGT2001) + P2*(WGT2003) + P3*(WGT2005) + P4*(WGT2007) + P5*(WGT2009) + e$, where Y is either *Student Reports of Safety*, *Student Reports of Peer Interactions*, or *Teacher Reports of Crime and Disorder*.

Level-2 Model

$P1 = B10 + r1$
$P2 = B20 + r2$
$P3 = B30 + r3$
$P4 = B40 + r4$
$P5 = B50 + r5$

Level-3 Model

$B10 = G100 + u10$
$B20 = G200 + u20$
$B30 = G300 + u30$
$B40 = G400 + u40$
$B50 = G500 + u50$

We then tested for whether the parameter estimates for G400 and G500 were statistically different. The estimates of G400 and G500, by school level and survey measure, are summarized in Table 11, along with the p-value of the differences of means tests.

Between 2007 and 2009, more significant changes in school safety occurred at the elementary school level. Elementary school teachers reported fewer incidents of crime and disorder and students reported more positive peer interactions during the 2008–09 as compared to the 2006–07 school year. While not reaching standard levels of statistical significance (e.g., $p<0.05$), elementary school students report feeling less safe in 2009 than in 2007. While there appears to be no difference in reports of crime and disorder among high school teachers, there is some evidence that high school students report more positive peer interactions in the 2009 survey. In addition, while not reaching standard levels of statistical significance (e.g., $p<0.05$), elementary and high school students, on average, report feeling less safe in the 2009 survey than during the 2007 survey.

TABLE 11

Survey Measure	School Level	G400	G500	p-value
Student Reports of Safety	Elementary School	5.88	5.85	0.07
	High School	5.38	5.32	0.07
Teacher Reports of Crime and Disorder	Elementary School	4.70	4.54	0.005
	High School	5.50	5.48	0.61
Student Reports of Peer Interactions	Elementary School	5.36	5.47	0.00
	High School	5.32	5.35	0.05

Appendix D:
Models of Safety by Neighborhood and School Context

TABLE 12

The share of variation in safety explained by neighborhood and school factors

Variation in Safety Explained by:	Student Perceptions of Safety	Teacher Perceptions of Crime and Disorder	Student Perceptions of Peer Interactions
Socioeconomic Context	0.510	0.404	0.554
… plus school context	0.646	0.519	0.631
… plus school achievement	0.759	0.655	0.715
… plus school leadership	0.762	0.704	0.725
… plus teacher collaboration	0.767	0.717	0.738
… plus school-family interactions	0.780	0.752	0.750
… plus student-teacher relationships	0.808	0.771	0.788
Number of Schools	524	387	524

Note: The share of variation in each of the three outcome measures relates to the R^2 from a regression. *Socioeconomic Context* includes poverty and crime in the student's home neighborhood and the extent of social resources in the community are measured by the CCSR student survey measure *Human and Social Resources in the Community*. School context includes controls for school racial composition, school enrollment during the 2008–09 school year and an indicator for whether the school is a high school or elementary school. The poverty and crime measures are based on the weighted average of the census block groups in which the students in the school live (weighted by school enrollment). School achievement is a composite of school-level math and reading achievement. See Table 10 for a list of the CCSR survey measures included in the School Leadership, Teacher Collaboration and Support, School-Family Interactions, and Student-Teacher measures. All variables have been standardized across all schools.

Endnotes

Introduction

1. Both "Zalisha" and "Lake Erie" are pseudonyms—school and student names were changed to protect confidentiality.
2. During the 2007–08 school year, the U.S. Department of Education found that 27.9 per 1,000 students in U.S. public schools reported being victims of violent crime while at school—violent incidents include rape, sexual battery other than rape, physical attack or fight with or without a weapon, threat of physical attack with or without a weapon, and robbery with or without a weapon (Neiman and DeVoe, 2009). This compares to a violent crime rate among the general population of 20.7 victimizations per 1,000 persons age 12 or older in 2007. Violent crimes include rape/sexual assault, robbery, and assault (aggravated and simple), and exclude murder (Rand, 2008).
3. During the 2007–08 school year, city schools experienced 35.8 violent incidents per 1,000 students, compared to 26.4 and 22.8 incidents per 1,000 students in rural communities and suburbs, respectively—violent incidents include rape, sexual battery other than rape, physical attack or fight with or without a weapon, threat of physical attack with or without a weapon, and robbery with or without a weapon (Neiman and DeVoe, 2009).
4. Neiman and DeVoe (2009).
5. Smokowski and Kopasz (2005).
6. Swearer et al. (2010).
7. Neiman and DeVoe (2009).
8. Harris Interactive and GLSEN (2005).
9. Neiman and DeVoe (2009). The survey identifies middle schools as those that serve students no less than fourth grade and no greater than ninth grade.
10. Source: Education Week online (retrieved from http://blogs.edweek.org/edweek/District_Dossier/2010/08/feds_to_tackle_bullying_at_con.html on September 2, 2010).
11. Macmillan and Hagan (2004); Bowen and Bowen (1999); Payne et al. (2003).
12. Schreck and Miller (2003); Macmillan and Hagan (2004).
13. Bowen and Bowen (1999).
14. Payne et al. (2003); Smith and Smith (2006); Allensworth et al. (2009).
15. Source: The Safe Schools/Healthy Students Initiative website (http://www.sshs.samhsa.gov/default.aspx (accessed July 15, 2009).
16. Source: The Safe Schools/Healthy Students Initiative website, http://www.sshs.samhsa.gov/default.aspx (accessed July 15, 2009).
17. Borum et al. (2010).
18. For example, a 10-year-old Florida student found a small knife in her lunchbox that her mother placed there for cutting an apple. The student immediately handed over the knife to her teacher; however, she was expelled from school for possessing a weapon (American Psychological Association Zero Tolerance Task Force, 2008).
19. Schreck and Miller (2003); American Psychological Association Zero Tolerance Task Force (2008).
20. Osher et al. (2010).
21. Dinkes et al. (2009).
22. Crosnoe et al. (2004).
23. Source: The City of Chicago official website, http://mayor.cityofchicago.org/mayor/en/press_room/press_releases/2010/june_2010/0622_cps_mentoring.html (accessed November 9, 2009).
24. An ecological theory of human development that comes out of the developmental psychology literature views youth academic and behavioral development in the context of multiple social domains that simultaneously influence youth experiences and outcomes (Bronfenbrenner, 1979; Bogenschneider, 1996). In the sociological literature, a social-organization perspective echoes ecological theory by explicating the complex and interrelated roles that micro domains—home, school, and community—play in a child's life, recognizing that these domains act as overlapping spheres of influence on youth outcomes (Epstein and Sanders, 2000). Recent work on school safety has argued that a social-ecological model is a particularly useful framework for understanding and addressing bullying in schools (Swearer et al., 2010) as well as for improving overall school discipline and classroom management (Osher et al., 2010).
25. Felson et al. (1994); Bowen et al. (2002); Welsh et al. (1999); Welsh et al. (2000); Payne et al. (2003).
26. In fact, Welsh et al. (2000) note that "close scrutiny" of school climate and community characteristics should be explored to better understand school disorder. In a recent special issue of *Educational Researcher* dedicated to school safety, researchers have called for more work focusing on the contributions of school context to school safety outcomes (Astor, Guerra, and Van Acker, 2010).
27. Astor et al. (2009).
28. Sergiovanni (2004); Bryk and Schneider (2002); Bryk et al. (2010).
29. Felson et al. (1994); Payne et al. (2003); Crosnoe et al. (2004).
30. Crosnoe et al. (2004).
31. Welsh (2000).

Chapter One

32. We use pseudonyms for all schools to protect their identity and the identity of students and teachers who were interviewed about their schools.
33. This description is based on observational research notes, not survey responses.
34. In the statistical analyses presented in this report, the area just outside of the school is defined by a census block area. In areas of the city where the population is dense, this is about one city block. In areas with less dense population, this is an area of a few city blocks.

35 These come from student reports at our case study schools and other middle and high schools that were part of the Focus on Freshmen study.
36 Allensworth, Ponisciak, and Mazzeo (2008).
37 See Appendix C for more details on changes in school safety between 2007 and 2009.

Chapter Two

38 Bowen and Bowen (1999); Brooks-Gunn et al. (1993); Bowen et al. (2002).
39 Sampson et al. (1997).
40 We use a student survey measure, *Human and Social Resources in the Community*, as the measure of community collective efficacy. This measure captures students' assessment of the extent of their trust in and reliance upon neighbors and community members, and whether they feel that adults in the community know and care about them. Students were asked how much they agree with each of the following six items about the community in which they live: (a) there are adults in this neighborhood that children can look up to; (b) adults in this neighborhood know who the local children are; (c) you can count on adults in this neighborhood to see that children are safe and do not get into trouble; (d) during the day, it is safe for children to play in the local park or playground; (e) people in this neighborhood can be trusted; and (f) the equipment and buildings in the neighborhood park or playground are well kept.
41 See Chapter 1, "Case Study Methods," for a description of the interview sample.
42 Statistical analyses suggest that the relationships of racial composition can be largely attributed to community poverty and crime, although it is not possible to completely separate them. After taking into account the degree of crime, poverty, and human/social resources in students' communities, there are no differences by school racial composition in teacher reports of safety, and Latino and African American schools no longer look different in terms of student reports of safety. This does not mean that real differences do not exist across schools serving student bodies with different racial composition; it only means that the differences correspond as expected with differences in students' neighborhood environments. Peer interactions remain more negative at African American schools, even after accounting for community characteristics.
43 For the quality of peer interactions, the racial composition of schools (e.g., the share of African American students) is at least as strongly related to safety as school achievement.
44 Bryk et al. (2010).
45 For students attending K-8 schools, fifth-grade achievement may have been affected by school safety in the primary grades.

Chapter Three

46 Each safety measure (SAFE, TSAF, PEER) was regressed on: suspension rate; imported crime; imported poverty; human social resources; dummies for school level (high school vs. elementary school) and racial composition; enrollment in August 2009; and a composite of math/reading achievement. The standardized coefficient between suspension rates and student reports of safety was -0.13; with teacher reports the relationship was -0.28, and with peer interactions it was -0.16; each coefficient was statistically significant at the $p<0.005$ level.
47 American Psychological Association Zero Tolerance Task Force (2008).
48 Bryk et al. (2010). School leadership is defined as the degree to which leadership is inclusive of teacher influence; the principal's involvement as an instructional leader, the extent to which programs in the school are coordinated and sustained, and the extent to which teachers trust and respect their principal. Teacher collaboration and trust is defined as the extent of shared commitment among teachers and the extent of professional development toward improving student learning, the extent of feedback teachers receive concerning their instructional practice and performance, and the extent to which teachers trust and respect their colleagues. The nature of school-family interactions is characterized by the extent to which parents and teachers support each other to improve the learning environment for students. Student-teacher relationships are defined by whether students feel safe with and listened to by their teachers, and the extent to which students believe that their teachers care about their learning and overall well-being.

Chapter Four

49 Newmann et al. (1992); Singh et al. (2002).
50 Punishments need to have meaning if they are to be effective (Kazdin, 2000).
51 Loeber and Hay (1997).
52 Meyers and Miller (2004); Forehand, Miller, and Dutra (1997); Graber, Nichols, and Lynne (2006).
53 Cullen et al. (2003).
54 Recent experimental evidence assessing the impact of such an approach in elementary schools in Hawaii and Illinois found improvements in student achievement and school safety (Horner et al., 2009).
55 More information is available from the U.S. Department of Education Office of Special Education Programs Center on Positive Behavioral Interventions and Supports (www.pbis.org).

About the Authors

Matthew P. Steinberg

Matthew Steinberg is a fourth-year doctoral student at the Harris School of Public Policy Studies at the University of Chicago and an Institute of Education Sciences Pre-Doctoral Fellow with the University of Chicago Committee on Education. His research is focused on urban education policy, exploring how the political economy of schooling as well as a school's social-organizational structure impact school climate and student cognitive and non-cognitive outcomes. Matthew received his BA in Economics and Sociology from the University of Virginia, an MSEd. in elementary education from the City College of New York and a Master's in Public Affairs from the Robert M. La Follette School of Public Affairs at the University of Wisconsin-Madison. Previously, Matthew was an investment banker and a New York City Teaching Fellow, teaching fifth grade in a low-income New York City community.

Elaine M. Allensworth

Elaine Allensworth, Ph.D. is Senior Director and Chief Research Officer at the Consortium on Chicago School Research at the University of Chicago. She is best known for her research on early indicators of high school graduation, college readiness and the transition from middle to high school. Her work on early indicators of high school graduation has been adopted for tracking systems used in Chicago and other districts across the country, and is the basis for a tool developed by the National High School Center. She is one of the authors of the book Organizing Schools for Improvement: Lessons from Chicago, which provides a detailed analysis of school practices and community conditions that promote school improvement. Currently, she is working on several studies of high school curriculum funded by the Institute of Education Sciences at the U.S. Department of Education and the National Science Foundation. She recently began a study of middle grade predictors of college readiness, funded by the Bill and Melinda Gates Foundation. Dr. Allensworth holds a Ph.D. in Sociology, an M.A. in Urban Studies from Michigan State University, and was once a high school Spanish and science teacher.

David W. Johnson

David W. Johnson is a research assistant at the Consortium on Chicago School Research and a doctoral candidate at the University of Chicago's School of Social Service Administration. His dissertation research describes and analyzes the role of school culture and climate in high school reform efforts targeting college enrollment and persistence. His current research also includes studies on the postsecondary transitions of low-income, minority students in the International Baccalaureate Programme and a large-scale, longitudinal study of college match. Prior to joining CCSR, David taught elementary school in the Washington DC Public Schools. David holds an AM in Social Service Administration and a M.Div. from the Divinity School at the University of Chicago. He received his A.B. in Philosophy and Germanic Languages & Literatures from Washington University in St. Louis.

This report reflects the interpretation of the authors. Although CCSR's Steering Committee provided technical advice and reviewed earlier versions, no formal endorsement by these individuals, organizations, or the full Consortium should be assumed.

This report was produced by CCSR's publications and communications staff.

Editing by Ann Lindner
Graphic Design by Jeff Hall Design
Photos by David Schalliol

5-11/.5M/jh.design

Consortium on Chicago School Research

Directors

Paul D. Goren
Lewis-Sebring Director
Consortium on Chicago School Research

Elaine M. Allensworth
Senior Director and Chief Research Officer
Consortium on Chicago School Research

Melissa Roderick
Hermon Dunlap Smith Professor
School of Social Service Administration
University of Chicago

Penny Bender Sebring
Founding Director
Consortium on Chicago School Research

Steering Committee

Ruanda Garth McCullough, *Co-Chair*
Loyola University, Chicago

Arie J. van der Ploeg, *Co-Chair*
American Institutes for Research

Institutional Members

Clarice Berry
Chicago Principals and Administrators Association

Sarah Kremsner
Chicago Public Schools

Karen Lewis
Chicago Teachers Union

Connie J. Wise
Illinois State Board of Education

Individual Members

Veronica Anderson
Stanford University

Amie Greer
Vaughn Occupational High School-CPS

Cornelia Grumman
Ounce of Prevention

Timothy Knowles
Urban Education Institute

Dennis Lacewell
Urban Prep Charter Academy for Young Men

Lila Leff
Umoja Student Development Corporation

Peter Martinez
University of Illinois at Chicago

Gregory Michie
Concordia University of Chicago

Brian Spittle
DePaul University

Matthew Stagner
Chapin Hall Center for Children

Luis R. Soria
Ellen Mitchell Elementary School

Kathleen St. Louis
The Chicago Public Education Fund

Amy Treadwell
Teach Plus Chicago

Josie Yanguas
Illinois Resource Center

Kim Zalent
Business and Professional People for the Public Interest

Steve Zemelman
Illinois Writing Project

Our Mission

The Consortium on Chicago School Research (CCSR) at the University of Chicago conducts research of high technical quality that can inform and assess policy and practice in the Chicago Public Schools. We seek to expand communication among researchers, policymakers, and practitioners as we support the search for solutions to the problems of school reform. CCSR encourages the use of research in policy action and improvement of practice, but does not argue for particular policies or programs. Rather, we help to build capacity for school reform by identifying what matters for student success and school improvement, creating critical indicators to chart progress, and conducting theory-driven evaluation to identify how programs and policies are working.

www.ingramcontent.com/pod-product-compliance
Lightning Source LLC
Chambersburg PA
CBHW060819090426
42738CB00002B/42